THE **BIBLE**

BOOK BY BOOK

THE BIBLE

BOOK BY BOOK

An Introduction to Bible Synthesis

G. Coleman Luck

MOODY PRESS
CHICAGO

ISBN: 0-8024-0045-0

29 30

Printed in the United States of America

INTRODUCTION

I. DEFINITION OF SYNTHESIS

1. Synthesis (or "the synthetic method") is derived from two Greek words which means "a putting together" or "a placing together." The word is opposite to "analysis" which means "a taking apart."

2. *Purpose*

In synthesis we approach a book of the Bible as a single unit and seek to understand its message *as a whole*. In this method it is not our purpose to examine small details but rather to get the broad sweep of the book and its general application, a bird's-eye view. On the contrary the analytical method involves a detailed examination of the text, "a taking apart."

3. *Procedure*

Each book of the Bible is to be considered separately. First introductory thoughts will be considered concerning the authorship of the book, the original recipients (if known), reasons for its being written, its theme, and so on. Then the attempt will be made to distinguish the principal divisions of the book in brief outline form, and the general contents of each of these main divisions explored. Each book of the Bible should be read at least three times in connection with such a study; once to note the main theme; the second time to observe the development of that theme; and the third to make an outline of the principal divisions.

II. THE BIBLE AS A WHOLE

1. *Authors*

On the human side it was written by about 36 or 40 men from various walks of life and over a space of 1500 years, from Moses to the apostle John. However, the true Author was the Holy Spirit of God (II Peter 1:21; II Tim. 3:16; Heb. 1:1, 2). All the human authors claim to be writing not their own words but the Word of God (see Exod. 34:27; Jer. 35:1, 2). Many times the expression "thus saith the Lord" or its equivalent is used.

2. *Recipients*

Written both to believers (I John 5:13) and to unbelievers (John 20:31).

3. *Date*

Written over a period of 1500 years, from the time of Moses (1440 B.C.) to the closing days of the apostle John (90 A.D.). So far as subject material is concerned the Bible takes us from eternity past before Creation (John 1:1) to eternity future (Rev. 22:5).

4. *Purpose of the Bible*

To reveal God and His purposes to men. The

supreme purpose, the glory of God (I Chron. 16: 27-29).

5. *Theme of the Bible*

Christ Himself (Luke 24:27; II Cor. 3:18; 4:6; cf. James 1:22-25).

III. THE PLACE OF THE OLD TESTAMENT

1. *Reason for Its Being Written* (I Cor. 10:11; "Now all these things happened unto them"—history; "for ensamples"—literally, "types"—typology; "and they are written for our admonition"—exhortation; "upon whom the ends of the world [lit. ages] are come"—dispensational teaching).

2. *Distinguishing Characteristic—Law* (John 1: 17)

3. *Divisions*

    a. In the Hebrew Bible: Law, Prophets, Writings

    b. According to subject matter

       1) Law (Gen.—Deut.)

       2) Historical books (Joshua—Esther)

       3) Poetical books (Job—Song of Sol.)

       4) Prophetical books (Isaiah—Malachi)

    c. According to dispensations

       1) Innocence (Gen. 1:27—3:6)

       2) Conscience (Gen. 3:7—8:19)

       3) Human government (Gen. 8:20—11:9)

       4) Promise (Gen. 11:10—Exod. 19:4)

       5) Law (Exod. 19:5—to close)

CONTENTS

THE OLD TESTAMENT

THE NEW TESTAMENT

Pentateuch

The word Pentateuch comes from the Greek word used in Septuagint Version meaning "five volumes."

Genesis to Deuteronomy.

1. *Authorship*

a. Though each book of the Pentateuch does not bear the signature of Moses, nevertheless several important parts are definitely ascribed to him (Exod. 24:4; Deut. 31:9, 24-26).

b. Later books of the Old Testament often speak of Moses as the author of the Pentateuch. Remember that the Jews spoke of all five of these books as "the Law." (For Mosaic authorship see Josh. 1:7, 8; I Kings 2:3; II Chron. 34:14; Neh. 8:1, 14; 13:1).

c. The New Testament likewise ascribes the Pentateuch to Moses (Luke 24:27, 44; John 1:45; 5:45-47; Acts 28:23). Against these references the claims of destructive critics of the Bible, which state that Moses did not write the Pentateuch but that it was written by various writers some long time after the time of Moses, are of no importance.

GENESIS

I. AUTHOR

Written by Moses (see Introductory notes on Pentateuch).

II. RECIPIENTS

Not specifically stated but presented originally to the people of Israel.

III. DATE

About 1440 B.C. Of events covered; about 2400 years (from the creation of man to the death of Joseph.) Chapters 1-11 cover about 2000 years; 12-50 about 400 years.

IV. PURPOSE OF THE BOOK

1. To furnish an account of the beginning of all things—of the universe (1:1); of man (1:26, 27); of the Sabbath (2:2, 3); marriage (2:21-24); sin (3:1-7); sacrifice (3:21; 4:1-7); nations (10:32); governments (9:6)

2. Especially to show the origin of the nation of Israel as God's peculiar people from whom the Redeemer would come.

V. THEME

The title is a Greek word meaning "origin"; so this is the book of origins or beginnings. Here we find the revelation of the one Almighty God who is all-powerful and all-wise, and of His relationship to the origin of the world, to man, to sin, to salvation. Genesis provides us, so to speak, the first chapter in the history of redemption and lays the groundwork for the rest of the Bible. It shows us that "God has to do with man; man has to do with God" (G. Campbell Morgan).

VI. KEY VERSE: Genesis 12:1-3

KEY WORD: *generations*—19 times; traces the chosen line of the woman's Seed (Genesis 3:15).

Outline of Genesis

After the Creation record in the first chapter, the book largely revolves around the biographies of six men. Though there is some overlapping, the lives of these men make a convenient way of dividing the book.

I. CREATION (Ch. 1)
   1:1—The original creation
   1:2—Earth in chaotic state
   1:3-31—Earth brought into its present condition in six creative days

II. ADAM (Chs. 2-5)
   Ch. 2—Adam and Eve created, placed in Garden of Eden and given a commandment about the tree of the knowledge of good and evil
   Ch. 3—The temptation and Fall
   Ch. 4—Cain murders Abel; descendants of the godless Cain; Seth is born
   Ch. 5—From Adam and Seth to Noah

III. NOAH (Chs. 6-11)
   Ch. 6-8—The Flood

Ch. 9—The Covenant with Noah and his sons;
Noah's prophetic blessing of his sons

Ch. 10—Beginning of the nations

Ch. 11—Men dispersed; the beginning of languages; the family of Shem to Abraham

IV. ABRAHAM (Chs. 12-23)

Ch. 12—The call of Abraham

Ch. 13—Abraham separates from Lot

Ch. 14—Abraham delivers Lot and is blessed by Melchizedek

Ch. 15—God renews and enlarges the covenant with Abraham

Ch. 16—A misstep, the birth of Ishmael

Ch. 17—Covenant confirmed and circumcision established as "a token of the covenant"

Ch. 18—Abraham pleads for Sodom

Ch. 19—Sodom destroyed but Lot rescued

Ch. 20—Abraham's faith falters at Gerar (as at Egypt 12:10-20)

Ch. 21—Birth of Isaac

Ch. 22—Offering of Isaac (Type of Christ)

Ch. 23—Death of Sarah

V. ISAAC (Chs. 24-27)

Ch. 24—A bride secured for Isaac. (An illustration of Christ and the Church)

Ch. 25—Abraham's closing days and the birth of Isaac's twin sons, Esau and Jacob

Ch. 26—The covenant confirmed to Isaac

Ch. 27—Isaac gives the blessing intended for Esau
to Jacob

VI. JACOB (Chs. 28-36)
Ch. 28—God speaks to Jacob at Bethel renewing
the covenant
Ch. 29—Jacob marries Leah and Rachel, working
seven years for each. Four sons born of Leah
Ch. 30—Seven sons and a daughter born to Jacob
by his two wives and two concubines
Ch. 31—Jacob, commanded by God to return
home, flees from Laban
Ch. 32—God wrestles with Jacob and he is changed
to Israel
Ch. 33—Jacob and Esau reconciled
Ch. 34—Jacob's daughter seduced and two sons
become murderers to avenge her
Ch. 35—Jacob returns to Bethel and has com-
munion with God there; Rachel dies at time
of Benjamin's birth; Isaac dies
Ch. 36—Esau's family—the Edomites

VII. JOSEPH (Chs. 37-50)
Ch. 37—Sold into slavery by his wicked brothers
Ch. 38—Judah's immorality; his sons
Ch. 39—Joseph becomes Potiphar's slave and is
cast into prison because of the false accusation
of Potiphar's wife
Ch. 40—Joseph interprets the dreams of Pharaoh's
butler and baker

Ch. 41—Joseph interprets Pharaoh's prophetic dream and is exalted to high position

Ch. 42—Joseph's brethren buy grain but do not recognize him; he arrests Simeon but allows the others to go back home

Ch. 43—They return the second time with Benjamin

Ch. 44—Joseph threatens to enslave Benjamin, and Judah pleads for him

Ch. 45—Joseph reveals himself to his brethren and sends them for Jacob

Ch. 46—Jacob and family move to Egypt

Ch. 47—The Israelites prosper in Egypt

Ch. 48—Jacob blesses Ephraim and Manasseh, Joseph's sons

Ch. 49—Jacob's prophetic blessing of his twelve sons

Ch. 50—Jacob's burial and Joseph's death

EXODUS

Introduction

I. AUTHOR

Moses. (See notes on Pentateuch; also Exod. 17:14; 24:3-7; 34:27, 28.) Writer evidently an eyewitness of events described.

II. RECIPIENTS

Presented originally to Israel but to be preserved by them for our admonition.

III. Date

Written during wilderness wanderings: 1440-1400
B.C. Covers about 215 years—from the going of
Jacob's family to Egypt to the giving of the law at
Mount Sinai. Note: From covenant with Abra-
ham (Gen. 12:1-3) to journey to Egypt, 215 years;
from then to Exodus 215 more years (Gal. 3:17).
Sir Charles Marston in *The New Knowledge about
the Old Testament* identifies Thotmes III as the
Pharoaah of the Oppression (1501-1447) and Amen-
hotep II as the Pharaoh of the Exodus (1447-1423).
The exodus took place about 1440 B.C.

IV. Purpose of the Book

To show how God's promise to Abraham (Gen.
15:12-16) was fulfilled in the triumphant delivery
of the children of Israel from their bondage in Egypt.
Also to record the origin of the Passover and the
giving of the law on Mount Sinai.

V. Theme

Title of the book used by Jews "these are the
names" after 1:1. But in the Septuagint called "Exodus." This Greek word used in Hebrews 11:22 of
this event. Also in Luke 9:31 of the death of Christ
and in II Peter 1:15 of Peter's death. So the book
tells of the bondage of the children of Israel in
Egypt, their redemption and subsequent instruction
in holy life and worship. There is a spiritual par-
allel in the life of each child of God: in bondage of

sin, redeemed from this bondage, then instruction
in holy life and worship.

VI. KEY VERSES: 3:8—God's purpose
       12:23, 29-31—Accomplishment of that purpose
       19:4-6—Instruction of those redeemed
       KEY WORD: *redeem*—10 times

Outline of Exodus

Possible outline: Historical Section (Chs. 1-18);
Legislative Section (Chs. 19-40). The following is
a longer outline based on events in the book. (Same
number of chapters in book as there were years of
wandering—forty!)

I. ISRAEL IN BONDAGE (Ch. 1)

II. ISRAEL DELIVERED (Chs. 2-14)

Ch. 2 A deliverer raised up but rejected when
         he first appears; Moses goes to Midian

Ch. 3 Moses is called to be Israel's deliverer but
         hesitates

Ch. 4 Moses raises two objections which are
         answered by Jehovah; he then returns to
         Egypt

Ch. 5 Pharaoh refuses to let Israel go but in-
         stead lays heavier burdens on them

Ch. 6 God renews His promise to Moses; the
         family of Moses

Ch. 7 Signs are shown to Pharaoh but he refuses
         to let the Israelites go. The First Judg-
         ment—river turned to blood

Ch. 8 Three more judgments placed on the
       land; two compromises offered
Ch. 9 Three more judgments
Ch. 10 Two more judgments
Ch. 11 The final judgment predicted
Ch. 12 The final judgment announced—death of
       the firstborn; way of deliverance provided
       for Israel—the Passover
Ch. 13 The firstborn set apart for the Lord; the
       journey begins under divine guidance
Ch. 14 Israel led through the Red Sea and the
       pursuing Egyptian army destroyed

III. The Journey to Mt. Sinai (Chs. 15-18)
Ch. 15 The Song of Moses; bitter water made
       sweet at Marah
Ch. 16 Hunger satisfied with quail and manna
Ch. 17 Water from the rock; victory over Amalek
Ch. 18 Moses' father-in-law gives advice

IV. The Law Given at Sinai (Chs. 19-24)
Ch. 19 The Law offered and accepted by the
       people
Ch. 20 The Ten Commandments
       Note the three divisions of the Law:
       The Commandments—express the will of
       God with regard to some all-important
       matters concerning the individual's re-
       lationship to God and man (Exod. 20)
       The Judgments—social regulations (Exod.
       21-23)

The Ordinances—religious ceremonials (Exod. 24-31)

Chs. 21-24 *The Judgments*
Concerning masters and servants, offenses punishable by death, compensation for injury to life and limb, property rights, penalty for theft, and many miscellaneous laws

V. THE TABERNACLE AND THE PRIESTHOOD (Chs. 25-40)

Chs. 25-27 Instructions given for building the Tabernacle
Observe its limited size (hardly larger than a room in some homes) ; its unusual purpose (not where fellow-worshipers could meet as in a modern church building, but where representatives of the people could meet with God) ; its wealth of typical teaching. These chapters give minute instructions for the materials, furniture, and arrangement

Chs. 28-29 Instructions regarding the priesthood: garments, consecration, methods of offering sacrifices, etc.

Chs. 30-31 Further details about the Tabernacle

Chs. 32-34 Parenthetical—the people worship the golden calf; Moses intercedes for them

Chs. 35-40 Tabernacle constructed from the plans previously given

LEVITICUS

Introduction

I. AUTHOR

Moses (see notes on Pentateuch. Also see 1:1, "The Lord called unto Moses." These or similar words are used about thirty-six times in the 27 chapters. Moses referred to by name fifty-five times in the book. (Also Cf. Matt. 8:4 with Lev. 14; Rom. 10:5 with Lev. 18:5.)

II. RECIPIENTS

1. Israel (see 1:2; 4:1-2; 7:23, 29; 11:2; etc.)
2. Especially Aaron and his descendents (the priests) (see 6:9; 6:25; 16:2; 21:1, 17; 22:2)

III. DATE

Passover took place on the fourteenth day of the first month (Exod. 12:2-3, 6). Tabernacle set up one year later—first day of first month of second year (Exod. 40:17). Numbers begins first day of second month of second year (Num. 1:1). Leviticus therefore given during the first month of the second year after leaving Egypt. This was about 1439 B.C.

IV. PURPOSE OF THE BOOK

1. It was written to show how God would fulfill His promise of Exodus 25:22
2. It was written to instruct Israel in the holy life which God expects of those who are His worshipers (11:45; 19:2)
3. It was written to provide instruction for the

Levitical priesthood as to the proper conduct of their office.   (See II-2)

4. It was written to provide prophetic illustrations (types) of the coming Saviour and the work He would accomplish (Heb. 10:1) .

Observe the title: Leviticus—from Septuagint, means "the Levitical book." Of course the priests were from the tribe of Levi (Heb. 7:11), but the Levites as such are mentioned only in 25:32, 33. Numbers deals more fully with the Levites; Leviticus with the priests.   In the Hebrew Old Testament it is called by the equivalent of the first three words: "And he called." These opening words *are* significant with regard to this particular book, as it contains God's call to worship and to holiness.

Note also the connection between the books already studied:

Genesis—man's creation and fall into sin; God's promise of a Redeemer and His choice of Israel as the nation through whom that Redeemer should come.

Exodus—Israel's deliverance from bondage; closes with the place of worship set up.

Leviticus—The proper method of worship given in detail.

V.   THEME: A holy people worshiping a holy God "in the beauty of holiness" (I Chron. 16:29) .

VI.   KEY VERSE: Leviticus 19:2

KEY WORDS: *holy* (plus *sanctify, sanctified,*

sanctuary, hallow, hallowed—all from same He-
brew root) used one hundred thirty-one times.
Key idea of this word is "set apart"
Sacrifice (with offering and oblation) about
three hundred times
Clean and unclean—about two hundred times
Atonement—thirty-six times

Outline of Leviticus

I. THE PROPER WAY OF APPROACH TO A HOLY GOD
     Chs. 1-10)
   1. Through Sacrifice (Chs. 1-7)
Here is a detailed statement concerning the five
different offerings which were to be made by Israel.
These offerings are a type of Christ; they contain
a typical description of what Christ has accomplished
for us.
   Sweet savor offerings—
   Ch. 1 The Burnt Offering
   Ch. 2 The Meal Offering; the only unbloody
          offering. Consisted of meal and oil, or of
          green ears of corn dried, and oil
   Ch. 3 The Peace Offering
   Non-sweet savor offerings—
   Ch. 4 The Sin Offering
   Ch. 5 The Trespass Offering
   Chs. 6-7 The Laws of the Offerings—Further in-
          structions as to how the priests shall handle
          each offering

2. *Through the Priesthood* (Chs. 8-10)

Ch.   8 The consecration of the priests (cf. Exod. 28, 29)

Ch.   9 The ministry of the priests begins

Ch. 10 Nadab and Abihu smitten because of offering "strange fire"

II.   THE PEOPLE OF GOD TO BE HOLY (Chs. 11-24)

Ch. 11 Their food

Ch. 12 Ceremonial purification in motherhood

Chs. 13-14 Purification in leprosy

    Ch. 13—Rules for judging whether person is clean or unclean, how to detect and diagnose leprosy

    Ch. 14—"The law of the leper in the day of his cleansing"

Ch. 15 Various rules of cleansing in private life

Ch. 16 The Day of Atonement—an annual time of national purification

Ch. 17 Their place of worship and their solemn prohibition—"eat no blood"

Chs. 18-20 The relationship of the people with one another to be holy

Chs. 21-22 Regulations for the priests (priests—holy; offerings—unblemished)

Ch. 23 The seven special seasons of worship (the annual feasts) :

    1. Passover—first month, fourteenth day (approx. April) ; speaks of the cross

2. Unleavened Bread—first month, fifteenth to twenty-first days; speaks of holy life after conversion

3. First fruits—at the beginning of the barley harvest; type of resurrection of Christ

4. Wave loaves—fifty days after first fruits. Speaks of Pentecost, beginning of Church

5. Trumpets—First day of the seventh month (about our October); typical of the coming of the Lord and the regathering of Israel

6. Day of Atonement—tenth day of the seventh month (see ch. 16); speaks of atonement for Israel (Zech. 13:1; Rom. 11:26)

7. Tabernacles—fifteenth to twenty-first days of the seventh month; refers to millennial blessing; Israel restored to separated place

Ch. 24 Instructions for oil and showbread; penalty for blasphemy

III. THE LAW OF THE LAND OF GOD (Chs. 25-26)
   Ch. 25 The Sabbatic year; the year of Jubilee; provision for the poor
   Ch. 26 General promises and warnings

IV. VOWS TO GOD (Ch. 27)

NUMBERS

Introduction

I. AUTHOR

Moses (see introductory notes on Pentateuch cf. also 33:1, 2)

II. RECIPIENTS

Mostly history and thus recipients not named. Sometimes Israel is mentioned (6:2; 15:2); or Aaron, the High Priest (8:2).

III. DATE

This book covers most of the wilderness wanderings of Israel—about 38 years, 9 months. (Num. 1:1; 33:38; 36:13; Deut. 1:3). Evidently written or at least completed at the close of this period, about 1401 B.C.

IV. PURPOSE OF THE BOOK

To record something of the 40 years wilderness wanderings of Israel brought on by their unbelief (14:32-34). Also to record the census of the two generations and to link them together in history (1:2, 3; 26:2). *In this connection the title* may be considered. It is the translation of the title in the Septuagint; the book is so called because it records the two numberings of the Israelites—before leaving Sinai and before entering Canaan. Title in the Hebrew Bible is "In the wilderness" (1:1), one word in Hebrew.

V. THEME

God's people divinely disciplined due to disobedience; or "wilderness experiences." Note these years of wandering are omitted in the record of Hebrews 11:29, 30. Many needed lessons were learned, but these painful experiences could have been avoided if they had been willing to step out in faith in the beginning. It was necessary for them to *pass through* the wilderness but *not* to spend 40 years there. (Remember there is a normal wilderness experience and an abnormal wilderness experience.)

VI. KEY VERSES: 14:28-30

KEY WORD: *wilderness*—45 times

Outline of Numbers

I. ISRAEL NUMBERED AT SINAI AND PREPARED FOR THE JOURNEY (Chs. 1-9)

(Time—20 days, cf. 1:1 with 10:11)

Ch. 1 The numbering of the host

Ch. 2 The arrangement of the camp preparatory to the march

East Side—Judah, Issachar, Zebulun (vs. 1-9)

South Side—Reuben, Simeon, Gad (vs. 10-16)

Center—Levites (vs. 17)

West Side—Ephraim, Manasseh, Benjamin (vs. 18-24)

North Side—Dan, Asher, Naphtali (vs. 25-34)

Ch. 3 Levites chosen for holy service, their charges assigned, and their number counted

Ch. 4 Further instruction regarding the service of the different families of Levites

Ch. 5 How to remove defilement from the camp

Ch. 6 The Nazarite

Ch. 7 Voluntary offerings of the princes

Ch. 8 Cleansing of the Levites

Ch. 9 First passover celebrated

II. FROM SINAI TO KADESH-BARNEA (Chs. 10-12)
   (Time: 11 days. Cf. Num. 10:11 with Deut. 1:2
—"Sinai" the peak; "Horeb" the range of mountains)

Ch. 10 The journey begun

Ch. 11 People complain at Taberah and are smitten by the Lord when they lust for the fleshpots of Egypt; quail and judgment are sent by the Lord at Kibroth-hataavah

Ch. 12 Miriam and Aaron complain against Moses; Miriam is smitten with leprosy

III. AT KADESH; *the Years of Wandering, Back to Kadesh* (Chs. 13-20)
   (Time—40 days; then 38 years. Num. 14:34.)

Ch. 13 Spies sent out to search out the promised land; they bring back an evil report

Ch. 14 The people refuse to enter the land through unbelief; condemned to 40 years in the wilderness by God

Ch. 15 Instructions to be observed when they enter the land (God's purpose unchanged)

Ch. 16 The rebellion of Korah and his companions

Ch. 17 Aaron's rod buds to prove he is God's chosen priest

Ch. 18 Further instruction concerning Aaron and the Levites

Ch. 19 The ordinance of the red heifer. (Speaks of cleansing from daily defilement.)

Ch. 20 Back to Kadesh; Moses sins and smites the rock the second time; Aaron dies

IV. Kadesh to the Jordan (Chs. 21-36)
(Time—6 months. Cf. Num. 33:38 with Deut. 1:3)

Ch. 21 Victory; complaint, fiery serpents. Serpent of brass raised (Cf. John 3:15)

Chs. 22-24 Balaam and his prophecies. Balak king of Moab tries to hire him to curse Israel. Instead he is forced by God to bless. Sublime Messianic prophecies are given

Ch. 25 Men of Israel commit whoredom with wicked women of Moab and are judged

Ch. 26 New generation numbered

Ch. 27 Joshua chosen to succeed Moses

Chs. 28-29 Various offerings ordered

Ch. 30 Instruction regarding vows

Ch. 31 Victory over the Midianites

Ch. 32 Reuben, Gad, and half of Manasseh choose land east of Jordan

Ch. 33 Summary of the journeys of the Israelites

Ch. 34 Instructions for dividing the land

Ch. 35 The Cities of Refuge

Ch. 36 Inheritance of each tribe to be secure

DEUTERONOMY

Introduction

I. AUTHOR

Moses (1:1; 31:9, 22, 24-27). His name is used thirty-six times in the book. Moses speaks in the first person in 1:16, 18; 3:21; 29:5. Old Testament writers refer a number of times to Moses as the author of Deuteronomy; for instance, II Chronicles 25:4; compare Deuteronomy 24:16. The Lord Jesus Christ spoke of Moses as the author of Deuteronomy (Matt. 19:7-9; cf. Deut. 24:1-4; John 5:45-47; cf. Deut. 18:15). He also accepted the statement of the Jews as to this: compare Luke 20:28 with Deuteronomy 25:5, 6. New Testament writers quote the book as from Moses; for example, compare Romans 10:19 and Deuteronomy 32:21. Words from Deuteronomy are quoted ninety times in the New Testament and in fourteen of the New Testament books.

In spite of this, the higher critics attacked this book first in claiming it was written four or five hundred years after the time of Moses.

II. RECIPIENTS

Israel, that is, the new generation that was to enter the promised land (1:1-3).

III. DATE

Covers approximately two months (Deut. 1:3; 34:5, 8; Josh. 4:19). It also contains a review of entire wanderings. Written about 1400 B.C.

IV. PURPOSE OF THE BOOK

Moses the great leader is about to die. The old generation has passed on now (2:14-16) except Caleb and Joshua. So Moses instructs the people and urges them to be faithful to their covenant with Jehovah. He also seeks to prepare them for their entrance, conquest and possession of Canaan.

V. THEME

Title (Heb. O. T.), "These are the words." Septuagint *Deuteronomion*—from Deuter—*second* and Nomos—*law*. However it is not a "second law" but rather a repetition and enlargement of the law previously given at Mount Sinai.

VI. KEY VERSES: 10:12, 13

KEY WORDS: *hear*—about 50 times
Do, keep, observe—a total of 177 times
Love—21 times (God's to man; man's to God; the basis for *do*)

Special Note: In answering Satan (Luke 4) the Lord quoted from this book alone (Deut. 8:3; 6:13; 6:16).

Outline of Deuteronomy

In this book we have the final messages of Moses to the Israelites just before they crossed the Jordan River into the promised land; also the closing scenes of his life and ministry.

I. THE FINAL DISCOURSES OF MOSES (Chs. 1-30)
   (Four discourses—they begin at chapters 1, 5, 27, 29)

   1. *The first discourse*—A review of Israel's journey from Horeb to the Plains of Moab (Chs. 1-4)

   Ch. 1 Review of the journey from Horeb to Kadesh

   Ch. 2 From Kadesh to Bashan—victory over Amorites

   Ch. 3 From Bashan (victory over Og) to Bethpeor

   Ch. 4 The people exhorted to keep the covenant of Sinai and reminded of God's faithfulness

   2. *The second discourse* (Chs. 5-26) —a review and enlargement of the law

   Ch. 5 The Ten Commandments restated and the people reminded of the experiences at Mount Sinai

   Ch. 6 Further warning to keep the commandments of the Lord

   Ch. 7 Complete separation from the wicked Canaanites commanded, and victory over them promised

Chs. 8-13 Sundry warnings and exhortations

Ch. 14 Laws of diet—God's people must eat clean food.

Ch. 15 The sabbatical year (repetition of Exod. 23)

Ch. 16 The three national feasts (Exod. 23)

Ch. 17 Instructions regarding a king

Ch. 18 Moses' great Messianic prophecy

Ch. 19 Law repeated regarding cities of refuge

Ch. 20 Instructions regarding warfare

Chs. 21-25 Various regulations—inquest for murdered; marriage to captive, treatment of incorrigible children, etc. (ch. 21)—Law of divorce (ch. 24)

Ch. 26 Offering of first fruits

3. *The third discourse*: Blessings and curses (Chs. 27-28)

Chs. 27-28 Blessings and curses from Mount Ebal and Mount Gerizim. These two high mountains stand on each side of a valley where Shechem is located. Levites stood in middle of valley, some people on each side, on (probably) lower spurs of these mountains.

4. *The fourth discourse*: The covenant concerning the land (the Palestinian Covenant; chs. 29-30)

Ch. 29 Introduction to the covenant

Ch. 30 The Covenant itself. If the people are
       disobedient they will be driven from the
       land, but will be restored upon their re-
       pentance

II. CLOSING SCENES OF MOSES' LIFE AND MINISTRY
    (Chs. 31-34)
    Ch. 31 The book completed
    Ch. 32 The song sung
    Ch. 33 The blessing given
    Ch. 34 The life ended. This chapter evidently
           not written by Moses; it is thought Joshua
           wrote the first eight verses, and Ezra the
           last four

JOSHUA

Introduction

I. AUTHORSHIP

Uncertain. Traditionally thought among the Jews to be Joshua himself (1:1, cf. Lev. 1:1 and Num. 1:1; Joshua 24:26; I Kings 16:34). Christian writers, both ancient and modern, have generally been of this opinion. Some have suggested that it may have been written by Eleazar, the son of Aaron, or by Phinehas, the grandson. Must have been written by one who was present at the crossing of the Jordan (5:1) and while Rahab was still alive (6:25).

II. RECIPIENTS

As in other historical books, not specifically named.

III. DATE

About 30 years are covered by this book; from the death of Moses to the death of Joshua. Joshua was probably born about the time Moses fled from Egypt; hence he was forty years younger than Moses, or 80 when he took command. (Cf. Caleb, 14:7, 10.) Joshua died at 110 (24:29). Date of writing: completed about the time of Joshua's death, 1370 B.C.

IV. PURPOSE OF THE BOOK

To show how God's promises were fulfilled in the giving of the promised land to Israel (23:14), and also to show how Israel failed to fully possess the land (18:3).

V. THEME

The conquest and division of the land of Canaan (11:23; 21:43).

VI. KEY VERSES: 1:2, 3

KEY WORDS: *Possess* and *possession*—22 times
Inherit and *inheritance*—63 times

Outline of Joshua

I. ENTERING THE LAND (Chs. 1-5)

Ch. 1 Preparation to cross the Jordan and enter the land

Ch. 2 Rahab saves the two spies

Ch. 3 The Jordan miraculously crossed

Ch. 4 The memorial stones

Ch. 5 The new generation circumcised at Gilgal; the manna ceases; the Lord, the real leader, appears to Joshua

II. CONQUERING THE LAND (Chs. 6-12)

(Central part of the land conquered: 6-9)

Ch. 6 Jericho miraculously conquered

Ch. 7 Israelites defeated at Ai because of Achan's sin

Ch. 8 Ai captured

Ch.   9 Alliance made with the Gibeonites
          (Southern part of land conquered—10)
Ch. 10 Confederacy of southern kings defeated at
          Gibeon
          Brief review of conquest of south country
          in verses 28-43
          (Northern part of land conquered—11-12)
Ch. 11 Confederacy of northern kings defeated at
          Merom
Ch. 12 Summary of the kings conquered

III. DIVIDING THE LAND (Chs. 13-22)
Ch. 13 The portion of the two and a half tribes
          east of the Jordan
Ch. 14 Caleb asks for Hebron
Ch. 15 The portion of Judah
Ch. 16 The portion of Ephraim
Ch. 17 The portion of Manasseh (west of Jordan)
          half tribe
Chs. 18, 19 The portion of the other seven tribes
Ch. 20 Further instruction about the cities of
          refuge
Ch. 21 Cities for the Levites
Ch. 22 The altar of the two and a half tribes
          east of Jordan

IV. THE LAST MESSAGE OF JOSHUA (Chs. 23-24)
Ch. 23 A message of separation
Ch. 24 A message on service

JUDGES

Introduction

I. AUTHORSHIP

Uncertain. According to Jewish tradition (Talmud), Samuel was the author. The book must have have been written before David's conquest of Jerusalem (1:21). Also it seems to have been written *after* the establishment of the kingdom, because of the statement "in those days there was no king in Israel" (17:6; 18:1; 19:1; 21-25). This would pin the time of writing down to the reign of Saul or the early part of David's reign.

II. RECIPIENTS

As in other historical books, not specifically stated.

III. DATE

Time covered—about 300 years, from death of Joshua to death of Samson (1370 B.C.—1070 B.C.). (See I Kings 6:1.)

IV. PURPOSE OF BOOK

1. To continue the history of Israel, the chosen nation, from the death of Joshua to the time of Samuel.

2. To provide a terrible demonstration of the moral depravity of man by showing what happens when "every man does that which is right in his own eyes" (17:6; 21:25).

V. THEME

A brief history of Israel during the period of the

judges—men whom God raised up not merely for judicial matters, but to be leaders and deliverers of Israel before that nation had a king. At various times during this period Israel was given over into the hands of their enemies because of their sinfulness; but then God would raise up a deliverer and they would enjoy a period of peace, after which they would corrupt themselves again (2:14-19).

VI. KEY VERSES: 2:14-19

KEY WORDS: *Evil*—14 times (most of these *"did evil"*)

Judge (plus *judged, judgment*)—22 times

Outline of Judges

I. FAILURE AND JUDGMENT (Chs. 1-2)

Ch. 1 Failure of various tribes because of disobedience, compromise, and worldly alliance. (Partial failure of eight tribes pictured—Reuben, Simeon, Issachar and Gad not mentioned here.)

Ch. 2 Disobedience, judgment, and the institution of judges.

(Note the sad cycle of their experience, which was often repeated: sin, judgment, repentance, deliverance, then again into sin.)

II. THE TWELVE JUDGES OF ISRAEL (Chs. 3-16)

Ch. 3 (1) Othniel—nephew of Caleb; leads to victory over king of Mesopotamia

(2) Ehud—delivers Israel from oppression
of Moabites

(3) Shamgar—delivers Israel from the Philistines

Chs. 4, 5 (4) Deborah (with Barak)—defeats Jabin, king of Canaan and his captain Sisera; the song of victory in chapter 5

Chs. 6-8 (5) Gideon—he and his three hundred defeat the host of the oppressing Midianites

Ch. 9 Abimelech—wicked son of Gideon murders his brothers and makes himself a king for three years.

Ch. 10 (6) Tola and (7) Jair, of whom little is known, judge Israel

Ch. 11 (8) Jephthah the Gileadite — defeats the Ammonites

Ch. 12 (9) Ibzan, (10) Elon, and (11) Abdon—little known about them or their judging Israel

Ch. 13-16 (12) S a m s o n — w i t h supernatural strength defeats the Philistines and judges Israel but through lack of separation comes to an untimely end

III. APPENDIX ILLUSTRATING THE CONFUSION AND CORRUPTION OF THE PERIOD (Chs. 17-21)

Chs. 17-18 Idolatry. This goes back to beginning of period. The Danites, seeking more land, steal Micah's idols and false priest

Chs. 19-21 Immorality and civil war. Men of Benjamin, living in Gibeah, foully abuse and murder a traveling Levite's wife (ch. 19). The other tribes, being notified of the evil deed by the Levite, order Benjamin to produce the guilty parties for punishment. Upon refusal, war follows. Benjamin wins the first two battles; is defeated in the third battle and almost wiped out as a tribe. Only 600 men left, who flee to the wilderness (ch. 20). The rest swear to give these men no wives and so blot out the tribe, but later repent and provide wives for the 600; two-thirds from Jabesh-Gilead, a city of Gad on the other side Jordan, which did not help in the conflict, the remaining one-third from dancers at Shiloh during a feast there (a poor way to salve their consciences) (ch. 21).

RUTH

Introduction

I. AUTHORSHIP

Uncertain. Possibly Samuel—after he had anointed David and knew that David would be king. (4:22).

II. RECIPIENTS

As in other historical books, not specifically stated.

III. DATE

Covers about ten years of time. Not known just when it occurred, other than "when the judges ruled" (1:1). Probably near beginning of period of judges. Time of writing about same as that of Judges.

IV. PURPOSE OF BOOK

(1) To give insight into the brighter side of life during the period of the judges. It relieves the picture of the preceding book, which might lead us to think all was black and all had deserted God.

(2) It was evidently also written to show something of the family of David, especially to show how Ruth, a woman of Moab, became his great-grandmother. It is one of two books in Bible named after a woman.

V. THEME

The story of Ruth, a woman of Moab, who chooses to serve the God of Israel, and is richly blessed by Him.

VI. KEY VERSES: 1:15, 16; 4:10.

KEY WORDS: *Kinsman*—14 times

Redeem—9 times

Same Hebrew word (Gaal; except *kinsman* in 2:1) —"Kinsman-Redeemer"

VII. SPECIAL NOTE

TYPICAL TEACHING—In Old Testament Israel a person, or an estate, sold into bondage could be redeemed by another if that person were a near kinsman, able, willing, and free from bondage himself. Boaz did this for Ruth and her estate. So in the New Testament we see Christ, our great Kinsman-Redeemer, fulfilling all these requirements, redeeming those who are sold under the bondage of sin.

Outline of Ruth

I. RUTH CHOOSES (Ch. 1)
II. RUTH LABORS (Ch. 2)
III. RUTH WAITS (Ch. 3)
IV. RUTH IS REWARDED (Ch. 4)

I SAMUEL

Introduction

I. AUTHORSHIP

Unknown. In the Hebrew Bible I and II Samuel formed just one book, which book was called "Samuel." A Jewish tradition held that Samuel was the author. This does not seem possible, however, since the events recorded go far beyond the life of Samuel (his death recorded in 25:1). David's death is not recorded in II Samuel, so the books appear to have been written while David was still alive. Possibly Gad or Nathan was the author (I Chron. 29:29).

II. RECIPIENTS

As in other historical books, not specifically stated.

III. DATE

Coverage of book—from birth of Samuel to death

of Saul. This must have been at least 110 years, for Samuel was old (8:1) when Saul first was made king, and Saul reigned for 40 years (perhaps 1110-1000 B.C.) Eli was probably contemporary with Samson.

IV. PURPOSE OF BOOK

To continue the history of Israel after the period of the judges, and especially to show the origin of the kingdom. An ethical purpose also—to provide good and evil examples (Rom. 15:4; II Tim. 3:16, 17). This shown by detail on God's dealings with Eli's family.

V. THEME

The history of Israel, the chosen nation, from the birth of Samuel to the death of Saul, especially showing how the kingdom began with Saul as first king, and David later chosen to succeed him.

VI. KEY PASSAGE: 8:19-22

    KEY WORD: (No very clear ones)

    Anoint—7 times

    Rejected—7 times

Outline of I Samuel

I. SAMUEL—PROPHET AND JUDGE (Chs. 1-7)

  Ch. 1 The birth of Samuel, an answer to prayer

  Ch. 2 Hannah's prayer; Eli's evil sons

  Ch. 3 Samuel's call from God

  Ch. 4 Judgment falls on Eli's evil sons; the Ark taken by the Philistines

Ch. 22 David gathers his mighty men; Saul murders the priests
Ch. 23 Saul pursues David and almost catches him
Ch. 24 David spares Saul
Ch. 25 Samuel dies; David and Abigail
Ch. 26 David again spares Saul
Ch. 27 David serves Achish of Gath
Ch. 28 Saul and the witch of Endor
Ch. 29 David almost fights against Israel
Ch. 30 David defeats the Amalekites
Ch. 31 Saul slain and his army defeated by the Philistines

II SAMUEL

Introduction

I. AUTHOR

Same as I Samuel, since the two books are one in the Hebrew Bible.

II. RECIPIENTS

Not specifically stated.

III. DATE

Covers almost all of the reign of David, that is, 40 years (I Kings 2:11). This would be about 1000-960 B.C.

IV. PURPOSE OF BOOK

To carry on the history of Israel from the death of Saul to the reign of Solomon, and to give a picture of the firm establishment of the monarchy during the period of Israel's greatest power and glory.

V. THEME
The history of Israel during the reign of David.

VI. KEY PASSAGE: 7:8-16
KEY WORD: *David*—about 280 times

Outline of II Samuel

I. DAVID REIGNS IN HEBRON OVER JUDAH FOR SEVEN YEARS (Chs. 1-4)
Ch. 1 His lament over Saul and Jonathan
Ch. 2 David reigns in Hebron over Judah; Ishbosheth over Israel
Ch. 3 Abner goes over to David and seeks to make him king over all Israel, but is murdered by Joab
Ch. 4 Ishbosheth is murdered

II. DAVID REIGNS IN JERUSALEM OVER ALL ISRAEL FOR 33 YEARS (Chs. 5-24)
Ch. 5 David king over all Israel; he captures Jerusalem and makes it his capital
Ch. 6 David brings the ark to Jerusalem
Ch. 7 The Davidic covenant
Ch. 8 David's victories
Ch. 9 David befriends Jonathan's son, Mephibosheth
Ch. 10 David's army defeats the Ammonites and the Syrians
Ch. 11 David's great sin—adultery and murder
Ch. 12 David repents and is forgiven, but his child dies

Ch. 13 Amnon assaults his half-sister Tamar, and is murdered by her brother Absalom in revenge

Ch. 14 David forgives Absalom

Ch. 15 Absalom rebels against David, causing him to flee from Jerusalem

Ch. 16 Absalom takes control of Jerusalem

Ch. 17 Absalom listens to false advice and allows David to escape (beyond Jordan to Mahanaim)

Ch. 18 Absalom slain and his forces defeated

Ch. 19 David returns to Jerusalem and gives Joab's position to Amasa

Ch. 20 Joab murders Amasa and defeats Sheba's revolt

Ch. 21 David and the Gibeonites; war with the Philistines

Ch. 22 David's song of thanksgiving for God's deliverance

Ch. 23 David's last words; roster of his mighty men

Ch. 24 David sins by numbering the people

I KINGS

Introduction

I. AUTHOR

Unknown. Ascribed by tradition (Talmud) to Jeremiah.

II. Recipients

Not specifically stated.

III. Date

Covers a period of about 126 years—from the death of David to the death of Jehoshaphat (about 960-834 B.C.)

IV. Purpose of Book

In the Hebrew I and II Kings formed one book (as Samuel and Chronicles). The purpose of this book (I and II Kings) is to trace the history of Israel from the period of its greatest prosperity to its decline and fall, from the death of David to the Babylonian captivity. No doubt the author also had an ethical purpose—to show us how little man is able to rule himself.

V. Theme

Solomon's glorious reign, the dividing of the kingdom after his death, and the history of the divided kingdom through the reigns of Ahab in the northern and Jehoshaphat in the southern.

VI. Key Verses: 2:12; 11:13

Key Words: *King*—about 250 times
Prophet—43 times

Outline of I Kings

I. The Reign of Solomon (Chs. 1-11)

Ch. 1 Adonijah attempts to seize the kingdom, but the aged David has Solomon anointed and confirms the kingdom to him

Ch. 2 David's last charge to Solomon, and his death; Solomon established on the throne

Ch. 3 Solomon's prayer for a wise and understanding heart is answered

Ch. 4 The administration of Solomon's kingdom; his wisdom

Ch. 5 Hiram helps Solomon prepare materials for the temple

Chs. 6-7 Solomon builds the temple. (The temple in arrangement was a reproduction of the tabernacle, but about twice as large.)

Ch. 8 Dedication of the temple (includes sermon and prayer of Solomon)

Ch. 9 The Lord appears the second time to Solomon; some of Solomon's projects

Ch. 10 The Queen of Sheba visits Solomon

Ch. 11 Solomon's apostasy; the Lord's judgment; Jeroboam's appointment

II. THE DIVIDED KINGDOM: REHOBOAM AND JEROBOAM TO AHAB (Chs. 12-16)

Ch. 12 The kingdom divided under Rehoboam; Jeroboam's sin

Ch. 13 A man of God prophesies against Jeroboam's altar

Ch. 14 Judgment prophesied on Jeroboam and his line; Rehoboam reigns in the southern kingdom

Ch. 15 Abijam (Abijah) and Asa reign over Judah; Nadab and Baasha over Israel

Ch. 16 Elah, Zimri, Omri and Ahab reign over
Israel

III. Elijah and Ahab (Chs. 17-22)
(Something new now—the prophet superior in
importance to the king.)

Ch. 17 Elijah appears and predicts three years'
drought; he is miraculously supplied at
Cherith and at Zarephath; raises the wid-
ow's dead son

Ch. 18 Elijah wins the contest with the prophets
of Baal; the people acknowledge Jehovah
as God and the rain comes

Ch. 19 Jehovah encourages the discouraged Elijah

Ch. 20 Ahab is granted two victories over the
Syrians, but sins by sparing the wicked
Ben-hadad

Ch. 21 Ahab and Jezebel murder Naboth for his
vineyard; after his doom is announced by
Elijah he gains a brief respite by humbling
himself

Ch. 22 Ahab, encouraged by false prophets, goes
with Jehoshaphat against the Syrians at
Ramoth-Gilead; he is slain in battle

II KINGS

Introduction

I. Author
Unknown, ascribed by tradition (Talmud) to
Jeremiah.

II. RECIPIENTS
Not specifically stated.

III. DATE
Covers a period of about 270 years (855-586 B.C.),
from the reign of Ahaziah of Israel (Ahab's son) to
the Babylonian Captivity. II Kings 25:27 takes us
about 26 years beyond the captivity.

IV. PURPOSE OF BOOK
See notes on I Kings.

V. THEME
The history of the divided kingdom from the
death of Ahab and Jehoshaphat to the final captivity.

VI. KEY VERSES: 17:7, 8, 18-23
KEY WORDS: *King*—about 340 times
Prophet—31 times

Outline of II Kings

I. THE MINISTRY OF THE PROPHET ELISHA, THE
SUCCESSOR OF ELIJAH (Chs. 1-13)
Ch. 1 Elijah predicts the death of Ahaziah
Ch. 2 Elijah translated to Heaven
Ch. 3 Elisha predicts miraculous victory over
Moab for the three confederate kings
Ch. 4 Elisha performs five wonderful miracles
Ch. 5 Elisha heals Naaman, the Syrian
Ch. 6 Elisha divinely protected against the Syri-
ans; they besiege Samaria
Ch. 7 The Lord miraculously drives away the
Syrian army

II. FROM THE DEATH OF ELISHA TO THE CAPTIVITY OF ISRAEL, THE NORTHERN KINGDOM (Chs. 14-17)

III. HISTORY OF THE SOUTHERN KINGDOM FROM THE
  CAPTIVITY OF ISRAEL TO THE BABYLONIAN CAP-
  TIVITY OF JUDAH (Chs. 18-25)

Ch. 18 Revival under good King Hezekiah of
    Judah; the Assyrians invade Judah

Ch. 19 Jehovah destroys the Assyrian army in an-
    swer to Hezekiah's prayer

Ch. 20 Hezekiah's illness and miraculous re-
    covery; closing events of his life

Ch. 21 The evil reigns of Manasseh and Amon

Ch. 22 Revival begins under good King Josiah

Ch. 23 Further reforms of Josiah; he is slain in
    battle by Pharaoh-nechoh of Egypt; his
    sons Jehoahaz and Jehoiakim reign under
    Pharaoh's control

Ch. 24 Jehoiakim becomes tributary to Nebuchad-
    nezzar; after his death Jehoiachin, his son,
    reigns three months and is carried captive
    to Babylon; his uncle Zedekiah becomes
    king and rebels against Nebuchadnezzar

Ch. 25 The final destruction of Jerusalem and
    deportation of the people to Babylon:
    Gedaliah is made governor over the rem-
    nant remaining, but is murdered by Ish-
    mael and the remnant flees to Egypt

I CHRONICLES

Introduction

I. AUTHOR

Probably Ezra. This is the Jewish tradition and fits well with evidence in the book itself. The writer seems to have done his work after the return from the Babylonian captivity (I Chron. 6:15; 3:19, 9:1-2). Chronicles closes at the very point where Ezra begins, indeed Ezra is a continuation of it. Chronicles centers around the temple worship, the priests and the Levites. This fits in with the fact that Ezra was a priest (Ezra 7:11). The Hebrew is also said to be similar to that of Ezra and Nehemiah.

II. RECIPIENTS

Not specifically stated.

III. DATE

The events described in the book cover a period of about forty years, from the death of Saul to the beginning of Solomon's reign. This would be about 1000-960 B.C. The date of writing was probably 450 B.C., approximately the same as that of the Book of Ezra.

IV. PURPOSE OF BOOK

In the Hebrew text I and II Chronicles formed one book (as Samuel and Kings). Chronicles begins with the death of Saul and goes on through the Babylonian Captivity so covers about the same ground as II Samuel and Kings. It is usually thought that a prophet (like Jeremiah) wrote Kings, while a priest (probably Ezra) wrote Chronicles. *Chronicles* centers around the temple worship, the priests and the Levites; therefore, of course, centers around Jerusalem and the southern kingdom. It does not have much material about the northern kingdom. Kings centers around the throne, the political history of Israel; has much more material about the northern kingdom, and much more about the prophets; Elijah and Elisha play a large part in Kings; Elisha is not mentioned in Chronicles and Elijah only once. Compare the four Gospels: each presents the same general period of history, but with a different emphasis from the other three.

The purpose of this book (I and II Chronicles) is to give a history of the house of David during the kingdom period, also of the temple and priesthood under that dynasty.

V. THEME

The reign of David and his temple arrangements.

VI. KEY VERSES: 29:26, 27; 28:11-19

KEY WORD: *David*—more than 180 times

Outline of I Chronicles

I. THE GENEALOGIES (Chs. 1-9)

    Ch. 1 From Adam to Jacob and Esau, plus the family of Esau

    Ch. 2 The sons of Jacob and the descendants of Judah to the time of David

Note: The complete genealogies of all the people were kept in the court archives of Israel and Judah (9:1). These selections are not meant to be exhaustive, but rather reveal God's choice throughout the centuries.

II. THE TRAGIC END OF SAUL'S REIGN (Ch. 10)

III. THE CROWNING OF DAVID AND HIS REIGN AS KING OF ISRAEL (Chs. 11-21)

Ch. 14 David's victories over the Philistines and his fame

Ch. 15 David finally brings the ark to Jerusalem

Ch. 16 David's celebration at the time of the ark's return

Ch. 17 David's desire to build the temple and God's reply

Ch. 18 David reigns supreme

Ch. 19 David's victories over the Ammonites and Syrians

Ch. 20 David's further victories over the Ammonites and the Philistines

Ch. 21 David's sin in numbering the people and his punishment

IV. THE PREPARATIONS FOR THE BUILDING OF THE TEMPLE (Chs. 22-29)

Ch. 22 David prepares the materials for the temple and instructs Solomon

Ch. 23 David numbers and organizes the Levites for their temple service

Ch. 24 David organizes the priests

Ch. 25 David organizes the temple musicians

Ch. 26 David organizes other temple workers

Ch. 27 David's civil and military authorities

Ch. 28 David's closing message to the people at the time of the giving of the temple plans to Solomon

Ch. 29 Continuation of chapter 28: David's last

> words; Solomon is enthroned and David dies

II CHRONICLES

Introduction

I. AUTHOR
See notes on I Chronicles.

II. RECIPIENTS
See notes on I Chronicles.

III. DATE
Events described in the book cover a period of approximately 424 years, from the beginning of Solomon's reign to the decree of Cyrus for the rebuilding of Jerusalem (960-536 B.C.) For time of writing see notes on I Chronicles.

IV. PURPOSE OF BOOK
See notes on I Chronicles.

V. THEME
The history of Judah and Jerusalem from the reign of Solomon to the decree of Cyrus. I Chronicles reveals the deep desire of David to build the temple; II Chronicles records the sad departure of the people from that temple and its worship.

VI. KEY VERSES: 1:1; 5:1, 36:14, 17-18
KEY WORDS: *House* (referring to the temple, "house of the Lord," "house of God.") —about 148 times

Priest (and *priests*) —more than 80 times

Outline of II Chronicles

I. THE REIGN OF KING SOLOMON (Chs. 1-9)

Ch. 1 Solomon's first vision of God

Ch. 2 Solomon makes final preparations for building the temple

Ch. 3 Solomon builds the temple

Ch. 4 Solomon constructs the equipment for the temple

Ch. 5 Solomon dedicates the temple: the ark is brought in

Ch. 6 Solomon dedicates the temple: his sermon and prayer

Ch. 7 Solomon dedicates the temple: the sacrifices and the feast; Solomon's second vision of God

Ch. 8 Solomon's activities

Ch. 9 Solomon visited by the Queen of Sheba who beholds his wisdom and his wealth; he dies after reigning forty years

II. THE REIGN OF THE KINGS OF JUDAH FROM REHOBOAM TO THE BABYLONIAN CAPTIVITY (Chs. 10-36)

Ch. 10 The nation is divided at the beginning of Rehoboam's reign

Ch. 11 Rehoboam strengthens his kingdom

Ch. 12 Rehoboam is punished by God for his unfaithfulness; he dies after reigning 17 years

Ch. 13 The reign of Abijah and his war with Jeroboam

Ch. 14 The good beginning of Asa's reign

Ch. 15 The reformation under Asa

Ch. 16 The failure of Asa and his death

Ch. 17 Prosperity and revival during the reign of Jehoshaphat

Ch. 18 Jehoshaphat allies himself with the wicked Ahab

Ch. 19 Jehoshaphat is rebuked by the prophet; further revival during his reign

Ch. 20 Judah invaded during Jehoshaphat's reign but deliverance is granted

Ch. 21 Reign of the wicked Jehoram

Ch. 22 Wicked Ahaziah reigns briefly; Athaliah destroys all the princes but Joash

Ch. 23 Joash becomes king and Athaliah is executed

Ch. 24 The temple is repaired, but apostasy follows the death of High Priest Jehoiada; Joash is assassinated

Ch. 25 The reign of Amaziah and his wars with Edom and Israel

Ch. 26 The good reign of Uzziah finally marred by his transgression against the Lord

Ch. 27 Jotham reigns well, but the people still apostatize

Ch. 28 Reign of the wicked Ahaz

Ch. 29 Revival comes under Hezekiah

Ch. 30 The great Passover celebration under Hezekiah

Ch. 31 Further reformation under Hezekiah

Ch. 32 Hezekiah delivered by God from the Assyrian invasion

Ch. 33 Manasseh reigns wickedly, but reforms after an imprisonment in Babylon; his evil son Amon reigns for two years and is then assassinated

Ch. 34 The reformation under good King Josiah

Ch. 35 The great Passover celebration during Josiah's reign; he is slain in a battle with the king of Egypt

Ch. 36 The evil reigns of the last four kings of Judah: Jehoahaz, Jehoiakim, Jehoiachin, and Zedekiah; the Babylonian captivity and the decree of Cyrus seventy years later

INTRODUCTION TO POST-EXILIC BOOKS

A brief review of the history of the children of Israel:

I. CALL OF ABRAHAM (Gen. 12:1-3), about 1870 B.C.

II. JACOB AND FAMILY MOVE TO EGYPT, about 1655 B.C.

III. ISRAELITES LEAVE EGYPT UNDER MOSES, 1440 B.C.

IV. THEY ENTER THE PROMISED LAND UNDER JOSHUA 1400-1370 B.C.

V. PERIOD OF THE JUDGES (OTHNIEL TO SAMUEL), 1370-1040 B.C.

VI. PERIOD OF THE KINGDOM (Saul to Zedekiah), 1040-586 B.C.
  1. United Kingdom (Saul to Solomon)
  2. Israel (Northern Kingdom)—Jeroboam to Hoshea. Ended in Assyrian captivity. Southern Kingdom lasted some 135 years longer.
  3. Judah (Southern Kingdom)—Rehoboam to

Zedekiah. Ended in Babylonian captivity. First captives carried away by Nebuchadnezzar, 606 B.C. Final overthrow of Jerusalem, 586 B.C.

VII. THE EXILE

1. Under Babylonian control to about 538 B.C.
2. Under Medo-Persian control (see Dan. 5:30-31), 536 B.C. through rest of Old Testament history.
3. Decree of Cyrus to allow the Jews to return and rebuild temple (II Chron. 36:22-23; Ezra 1:1-4; see also Isa. 44:28; 45:1, written 200 years previously, and Jer. 25:11; 29:10).

EZRA

Introduction

I. AUTHOR

Traditionally—Ezra, the chief character of the book (see 7:1, 11, 25, 28; 8:15, 16, 17, 21, etc.) "Ezra" means "the helper." He was a priest, the son of Seraiah (7:1-5). Also a scribe (7:6, 21). (Scribes copied Scriptures, also studied and interpreted Bible; sometimes called "lawyers" in N. T.) A very godly man (7:10).

II. RECIPIENTS

Not specifically stated.

III. DATE

Covers a period of about 80 years (536-456 B.C.): from the decree of Cyrus (1:1) to a time shortly

after Ezra's arrival at Jerusalem (7:1; 8:31; 10:17).
Written at close of these events.

IV. PURPOSE OF BOOK

To give a picture of the re-establishment of the
Jews in their land, after the Babylonian captivity.
Note two distinct returns recorded in this book:
the first under Zerubbabel (chs. 1-6), then 78 years
later the second under Ezra (chs. 7-10).

V. THEME

The restoration of Jerusalem and Judah after the
Babylonian captivity.

VI. KEY VERSES: 2:1; 6:21-22

KEY WORDS: *Go up, went up,* etc., used a number of times.

Jerusalem—47 times

Outline of Ezra

I. ZERUBBABEL LEADS THE FIRST RETURN FROM
EXILE AND REBUILDS THE TEMPLE (chs. 1-6)

Ch. 1 Cyrus issues his decree and a group of
Israelites prepares to return

Ch. 2 The exiles return to their land

Ch. 3 The altar is built and the temple foundation laid

Ch. 4 Samaritan opposition causes suspension of
the work for 2 years

Ch. 5 The work begun again, because of the
encouragement of Haggai and Zechariah

Ch. 6 King Darius confirms the decree of Cyrus,
and the temple is completed

Note: About 57 years elapse between the end of chapter 6 and the beginning of chapter 7. During this period the events recorded in the book of Esther took place. King Ahasuerus (Xerxes) of Esther had made an expedition into Greece but had been badly defeated. After his return he took Esther as his queen.

II. EZRA LEADS THE SECOND RETURN FROM EXILE AND RECALLS THE PEOPLE TO THEIR SEPARATED POSITION (Chs. 7-10)

Ch. 7 A second remnant prepares to return under Ezra's leadership

Ch. 8 The journey of Ezra and his company and their arrival at Jerusalem

Ch. 9 Ezra finds the people have lost their separated position and he carries the matter to God in a prayer of confession

Ch. 10 Revival comes and the people return to their separated position

NEHEMIAH

Introduction

I. AUTHOR

Nehemiah ("Jehovah comforts"), the son of Hachaliah ("Jehovah is hidden"). When first we see Nehemiah, he is the cupbearer of King Artaxerxes (Neh. 1:11; 2:1; Ezra 7:1). He was appointed governor of Judah (5:14; 8:9; 10:1), which position he held for about 12 years.

II. RECIPIENTS

Not specifically stated.

III. DATE

The book covers a period of around 12 years (2:1; 5:14; 13:6). This would be approximately 444-432 B.C.

IV. PURPOSE OF BOOK

The book begins about 12 years after the close of Ezra (Ezra 7:8; Neh. 2:1). A great revival had taken place at that time, but now we find the people in a very depressed condition again. Almost 100 years have now elapsed since the first return under Zerubbabel. The temple has been completed, but the people are persecuted by their adversaries and unable to rebuild the wall of the city (Neh. 1:3), a very essential means of protection. They are in "great affliction and reproach." Ezra is still present as a priest and teacher, but now Nehemiah comes as governor with official instructions to rebuild the city (2:5). The first step is to rebuild the walls (2:17). This book tells how, under Nehemiah, the walls are rebuilt and the people revived.

V. THEME

Rebuilding the walls of Jerusalem (1:3; 2:13, 15. 17; 4:6; 6:15; 12:27).

VI. KEY VERSES: 4:6; 6:15-16

KEY WORDS: *Wall* (and *walls*) —32 times
Build—23 times

Outline of Nehemiah

I. NEHEMIAH RETURNS TO JERUSALEM AND REBUILDS THE WALLS (Chs. 1-6)

Ch. 1 Nehemiah learns of the afflictions of the remnant and Jerusalem

Ch. 2 Nehemiah is sent to Jerusalem and makes his plans there

Ch. 3 Building the wall

Ch. 4 The work continues despite opposition

Ch. 5 The work hindered by selfishness and greed

Ch. 6 The wall completed

II. SPIRITUAL REVIVAL (Chs. 7-10)

Ch. 7 Nehemiah makes provision for rule in Jerusalem and finds register of those who returned with Zerubbabel

Ch. 8 Ezra teaches the law and the people celebrate the feast of tabernacles

Ch. 9 Revival comes

Ch. 10 A covenant is made to be faithful to God

Note seven provisions of this covenant: (1) Not to marry heathen (v. 30); (2) to observe Sabbath (v. 31a) (3) to observe Sabbatic year (v. 31b); (4) to pay temple tax (vv. 32, 33); (5) to supply wood for temple altar (v. 34); (6) to give the priests and Levites their due (vv. 35-38); (7) not to forsake God's house (v. 39)

III. FURTHER REFORMS (Chs. 11-13)

Ch. 11 Provision made for the repopulation of Jerusalem

Ch. 12 The dedication of the wall. (Apparently sometime after this Nehemiah leaves for Shushan and returns in ch. 13)

Ch. 13 Nehemiah's return to Jerusalem and his correction of disorders there

ESTHER
Introduction

I. AUTHOR

Possibly Mordecai (see 9:20). The Hebrew is similar to that of Ezra and Nehemiah.

II. RECIPIENTS

The Jews of the dispersion in the various parts of the Persian empire (9:20).

III. DATE

Events described in the book begin with the third year (1:3) of the reign of Ahasuerus (Xerxes) and close with the twelfth (3:7). This was approximately 483-474 B.C. Esther became queen 479 B.C. (2:16).

IV. PURPOSE OF BOOK

To show God's providential care for His people even in their dispersion; also to show the origin of the Jewish feast of Purim (9:26-28; 3:6-7).

V. THEME

The providential deliverance of the Jews from destruction through the agency of Esther and Mordecai

VI. KEY VERSE: 4:14

KEY WORD: *The Jews*—43 times

(The name of God is not used even once, but His hand is as clearly seen in this book as in any other in the entire Bible.)

Outline of Esther

I. ESTHER BECOMES QUEEN OF PERSIA (Chs. 1-2)

Ch. 1 Queen Vashti displeases King Ahasuerus and is dethroned

Ch. 2 Esther is made queen instead of Vashti

II. HAMAN PLOTS TO DESTROY ALL THE JEWS, BUT IS DEFEATED BY ESTHER (Chs. 3-8)

Ch. 3 Haman's wicked plot

Ch. 4 The mourning of the Jews and the communication of Mordecai to Esther

Ch. 5 Esther secures the favor of the king and his presence at her banquet

Ch. 6 Mordecai is honored and Haman humbled

Ch. 7 Haman is executed after his plot is revealed to the king by Esther at a. second banquet

Ch. 8 Mordecai is promoted to Haman's position and the Jews are empowered by the king to defend themselves against their enemies

III. THE DELIVERANCE OF THE JEWS AND THE FEAST OF PURIM (Chs. 9-10)

Ch. 9 The Jews are victorious over their enemies and the Feast of Purim is established

Ch. 10 The greatness of Mordecai during the remainder of Ahasuerus' reign

Introduction to Hebrew Poetry

"Critics by no means partial to the religious side of Scripture have recognized that in lyric poetry the Hebrew leads the literature of the world" (Prof. Richard G. Moulton, Ph.D., of the University of Chicago, and Cambridge University, England).

I. HEBREW POETRY IS LARGELY "LYRICAL" IN CHARACTER

It was originally written to be accompanied by music on the lyre. So *lyric* means appropriate for singing (note use now of "lyrics"). Lyric poetry is subjective in nature, having to do with the thoughts and emotions in the mind of the composer, with events being mentioned as they affect him. This contrasts with epic poetry, which is objective in nature, being a narrative of great events. When it is religious, as in the Bible, lyric poetry has to do with the thoughts and feelings of the writer as he thinks of God and as his heart goes up to God.

II. THE NATURE OF HEBREW POETRY

1. Not achieved by a repetition of sound (rhyme) nor by a repetition of accent (verbal rhythm) as usually is the case with our poetry.

2. Chief characteristic is "thought" or "sense rhyme." Some speak of it as "logical rhythm"

or "parallelism." Three chief kinds of parallelism:

    a. Synonymous—same thought repeated in different words (examples: Ps. 3:1; 9:1-2; 24:1-3; Job 3:3-6)

    b. Antithetic—ideas contrasted and so emphasized (Ps. 1:6; 37:9; Prov. 15:1; 13:1)

    c. Synthetic—thought added to or developed (Ps. 1:2; 19:7-9; Prov. 22:6; Eccl. 12:13-14)

  3. Other features sometimes found:

    a. Acrostic arrangements, the lines or verses begin with the Hebrew alphabet in regular order (Lam. 1, 2; Ps. 119)

    b. Repetition of a phrase or sentence at intervals sometimes called iterative parallelism (Ps. 107; 136)

III. THE PLACE OF POETRY IN THE OLD TESTAMENT

  1. Poetic selections are found many times in the prose books:

    Examples—

      Jacob's Blessing (Gen. 49:1-27)

      Song of Moses (Ex. 15:1-19)

      Song of the War Flame (Num. 21:27-30)

      Farewell of Moses (Deut. 32:1-43)

      Song of Deborah (Judg. 5)

      Song of Hannah (I Sam. 2:1-10)

      Song of the Bow (II Sam. 1:17-27)

      David's Last Words (II Sam. 23:1-7)

      (Note—A. S. V. prints these in poetic form.)

2. SIX POETIC BOOKS

   a. *Job*—a drama with various conversations between Job and his friends concerning the problem of suffering.

   b. *Psalms*—the inspired hymn book of Israel; David the chief author.

   c. *Proverbs*—wise sayings, instruction for the daily life.
      Solomon the principal author.

   d. *Ecclesiastes*—the vanity and futility of life lived on a worldly basis. (Set off as prose in the A. S. V., but similar in many parts to the poetry of Proverbs.)

   e. *Song of Solomon*—a love song of Solomon; speaks in a typical way of Christ and the Church.

   f. *Lamentations*—Jeremiah's song of lament over desolate Jerusalem.

Note—These books make up about 20 per cent of the entire Old Testament. According to Terry, nearly half of the Old Testament was actually written in the poetic style.

JOB

Introduction

I. AUTHOR

Probably Job himself (19:23-24). Note that Job was a real historical character (Ezek. 14:14, 20; Jas.

5:11). Job would have been best acquainted with all the facts, and as he lived 140 years after these events took place (42:16), he had ample time to write them down. Some have suggested Elihu (see 32:15-17) or Moses as possible authors.

II. RECIPIENTS
Not specifically stated.

III. DATE
Probably about the time of Abraham or a little earlier (2000-1800 B.C.). This is shown by:

Job's great age (cf. Gen. 11:32; the later patriarchs were somewhat shorter lived).

The religion of Job—sacrifices offered by head of household—indicates a patriarchal time

No reference to Mosaic law

No reference to any form of idolatry except the earliest type—worship of sun, moon, and stars (31:26-28)

No reference to the exodus or to the destruction of Sodom and Gomorrah but one to the flood (22:15-16)

IV. PURPOSE OF BOOK
To deal with the problem as to how the suffering of the godly can be reconciled with the justice and love of God. Job, a pious, godly man, suffers the loss of his fortune, family and personal health. His three friends "comfort" him by arguing that suffering is always the consequence of personal sin, therefore Job, since he is such a great sufferer, must be a

great sinner against God. Job, while not claiming sinlessness, replies that his suffering is out of all proportion to his faults. Afterward a younger man, Elihu, gives his opinion on the subject at some length. Finally Jehovah speaks, showing the majesty and wisdom of God and the littleness of man. In the end, Job has a new experience with the Lord and greater blessing than before.

V. THEME

Why do the righteous suffer?

VI. KEY VERSES: 2:3; 42:5, 6, 10

KEY WORDS: *Affliction*—11 times

Righteous (and *righteousness*)—21 times

Answered and said—32 times

Outline of Job

I. PROLOGUE (Chs. 1, 2)

Ch. 1 The godly Job is unjustly accused by Satan, who with God's permission destroys Job's fortune and family.

Ch. 2 Job is accused a second time by Satan, who now destroys Job's health, but in spite of this Job does not "sin with his lips"; his three friends come to comfort him.

II. JOB AND HIS THREE FRIENDS (Chs. 3-31)

1. *The first cycle* (chs. 3-14)

Job speaks, then each friend speaks, and in turn is answered by Job.

Ch. 3 Job curses the day he was born and longs for death.

Chs. 4-5 The first speech of Eliphaz: Job is guilty
and is being chastened by God for his sin.

Chs. 6-7 Job's answer to Eliphaz: He asks him to
point out the sin.

Ch.   8 The first speech of Bildad: Job is a hypocrite.

Chs. 9-10 Job's answer to Bildad: It seems that
God destroys the perfect with the wicked,
and Job knows not how to bring his own
case before God. If he could, he would
declare his innocence.

Ch. 11 The first speech of Zophar: Job is not
only a sinner, but is now lying; he de-
serves even more punishment from God
than he is receiving.

Chs. 12-14 Job's answer to Zophar: He already
knows such things as his friends are say-
ing. He cannot understand God's dealing
with him, but will nevertheless trust Him

2. *The second cycle* (chs. 15-21)

Each of the three friends again addresses Job and
is in turn answered by him.

Ch. 15 The second speech of Eliphaz: Repeats
the old charge that Job is a wicked man
and a hypocrite.

Chs. 16-17 Job answers Eliphaz: He is innocent
and his friends are "miserable comforters."

Ch. 18 The second speech of Bildad: The old
theme—the wicked always suffer.

Ch. 19 Job answers Bildad: God has overthrown him and for some unknown reason he cannot get justice, yet his faith rises to a sublime height.

Ch. 20 The second speech of Zophar: The wicked quickly come to a terrible end—implication is that Job must be one of this number.

Ch. 21 Job answers Zophar: Their argument is shown false by experience itself—the wicked often prosper.

3. *The third cycle* (chs. 22-31)

The first two friends speak once more and Job answers each again.

Ch. 22 The third speech of Eliphaz: Insists Job is a sinner and itemizes crimes which Job must have committed; urges repentance.

Chs. 23-24 Job answers Eliphaz: He longs to present his case before God but knows not where to find Him (ch. 23); gives instances of the wicked doing evil deeds with apparent impunity (ch. 24).

Ch. 25 The third speech of Bildad: Tries to show Job's rashness.

Chs. 26-31 Job's final answer: He absolutely maintains his integrity.

III. THE DISCOURSE OF ELIHU (Chs. 32-37)

Nearer the truth than those of the three friends. He rebukes them for not answering Job (32:3, 12), and Job for justifying himself rather than God (32:2). His argument is that suffering is not always for sin—God does sometimes afflict the righteous, but for the purpose of chastening them and preventing pride (33:19). After the chastening He will exalt in due time (36:5-7). He is great and does not explain His dealings to us (33:12-13). Good as all this is, it is evident that Elihu does not have the slightest inkling as to the real cause of Job's testing as described in chapters 1 and 2.

IV. JEHOVAH SPEAKS (Chs. 38-41)

Job has no answer to Elihu, so God now speaks, declaring in majestic terms His mighty power and wisdom, the implication being that man knows too little to attempt to explain all the mysteries of providence.

V. EPILOGUE (Ch. 42)

This must be considered along with the prologue (chs. 1-2) for the full solution of the problem. In the beginning we were shown that Job's trials were not a punishment but a testing. Now we find that the result is a new experience with the Lord, followed by greater blessing than before.

PSALMS
Introduction

I. AUTHOR

Of the 150 psalms, 100 have the author's name inscribed.

1. David, king of Israel—73 psalms

2. Asaph (I Chron. 16:4-5, 7, 37), a Levite, chief of the sacred musicians—12 psalms.

3. Sons of Korah (I Chron. 9:19), Levites who served in the temple during David's reign—10 psalms

4. Solomon, king of Israel—2 psalms

5. Heman (I Chron. 25:1, 5-6), Levite who served as a musician during David's reign—1 psalm

6. Ethan (I Kings 4:31), probably another musician under David—1 psalm

7. Moses—1 psalm

In addition, Psalms 2 and 95 are ascribed to David by the New Testament (Acts 4:25; Heb. 4:7).

II. RECIPIENTS

1. The Lord (3:7; 4:1; 5:1)

2. The righteous (33:1; 37:1, etc.)

3. Israel (78:1; 105:5-6; 106:4-7, etc.)

4 All mankind in general (1, 2, 4, 19, etc.)

III. DATE

From the time of Moses (Ps. 90), 1440 B.C., to the Babylonian captivity (Ps. 137), about 580 B.C.

IV. PURPOSE OF BOOK

1. Psalms was the inspired worship book of prayer and praise for Israel. The experiences of the child of God as he lives in the world are graphically depicted—his doubts, fears, longings, hopes, joys and sorrows.

2. The book also presents the proper method of

true worship—right attitude of heart toward
God, occupation with God Himself, and satis-
faction found in Him.

3. In addition, the experiences of the wicked are
also presented in contrast with the righteous,
along with their final doom.

4. Beyond all this it is a great book of prophecy.
At least 13 psalms are proved to be Messianic
by New Testament quotations (2, 8, 16, 22,
31, 40, 41, 45, 68, 69, 102, 110, 118). Many
others also undoubtedly refer to Christ. The
future glory of Israel, and of the world, also
are subjects of prophecy.

Over one-fourth of the Old Testament quotations in the New Testament are from the
Psalms.

V. THEME

The believer communing with his God through
prayer and praise.

VI. KEY VERSES: 33:1-4

KEY WORDS: *Praise*—176 times

Blessed (with *bless,* and *blessing*)—92 times

Outline of Psalms

The various psalms were written over a period of
many centuries as shown by the authorship. Some
unknown person finally collected them and divided
them into five books, each of which ends with a
doxology. While the order in which the psalms are

arranged undoubtedly has a significance, there is no general agreement as to just what this significance is. While we cannot say with authority just why each psalm comes where it does, we can detect a logical sequence in many places. Psalm 1 forms a suitable introduction to the entire book, while Psalm 150 provides a fitting conclusion. Psalms 22, 23 and 24 reveal Christ as the Good Shepherd (John 10:11), the Great Shepherd (Heb. 13:20), and the Chief Shepherd (I Pet. 5:4). Psalms 120-134 are "songs of ascents" (thought to have been used by the people as they traveled to Jerusalem to celebrate the feasts of the Lord, or on the steps of the temple). Psalms 93-100 and 103-107 are psalms of praise, while Psalms 145-150 are "hallelujah psalms."

BOOK I—PSALMS 1-41

Largely prayers of David (37 out of the 41). Note a few outstanding examples from this book:

Psalm—

1 The blessed man contrasted with the ungodly

2 The Coming King. First great prophetic psalms (Acts 13:33 and Heb. 1:5; 5:5).

   a. Rejection of the King (vv. 1-3)

   b. Establishment of the King (vv. 4-6)

   c. Reign of the King (vv. 7-9)

   d. Preparation for the King (vv. 10-12)

3-7 Trials and sorrows of the godly

8 The exaltation of the Son of Man—Messianic (Matt. 21:16; I Cor. 15:27; Heb. 2:6-9)

14 Total depravity

16 Death and resurrection of the Messiah (Acts 2:25-28; 13:35)

19 God's witnesses: creation (vv. 1-3); revelation (vv. 7-11); prayer after consideration of these (vv. 12-14).

22 Psalm of the cross (Matt. 27:46; Mark 15:34). David never had such an experience; altogether prophetic.

23 The Great Shepherd

24 The King of Glory (clearly Messianic though not so quoted in the New Testament).

31 Prayer for deliverance—Messianic (Luke 23:46)

32 Blessedness of the forgiven sinner. Probably written after David had confessed his great sin (see also Ps. 51).

34 The joy of God's saints

40 The obedient Messiah (Heb. 10:5-7)

41 The Messiah betrayed (John 13:18, 21-30). David's experience foreshadows that of Christ.

BOOK II—PSALMS 42-72

Nineteen of these are by David. General subject: the sufferings of the godly and their deliverance. Outstanding examples:

Psalm—

42 Soul thirst for God in a time of affliction

45 The glory and power of the Great King—
Messianic (Heb. 1:8)

51 Confession of sin and prayer for restoration

63 Longing for God in the wilderness

68 Song of deliverance—Messianic (Eph. 4:8)

69 The suffering of the Messiah—Messianic (John
15:25). Frequently quoted in New Testament.
Note that as in other cases, however, only
parts of it are applicable to Christ (v. 5, for
example)

72 The Righteous King and His glorious reign

BOOK III—PSALMS 73-89

Psalms emphasizing God's dealings with Israel
from the beginning of the nation to the final blessing. Outstanding examples:

Psalm—

73 The problem of the prosperity of the wicked

78 God's past dealings with Israel (from Egypt
to David)

84 The loveliness of God's house

89 God's faithfulness in keeping His covenant
with David

BOOK IV—PSALMS 90-106

The sufferings and afflictions of God's people to
end with the Lord's reign. Outstanding examples:

Psalm—

90 The eternity of God and the transitoriness of
man

91 Security of the believer

  96 Call to praise in view of the Lord's coming

100 Praise for God's goodness and mercy

102 The Messiah prays in His humiliation (see Heb. 1:10-12; 13:8)

103 The Thanksgiving Psalm

BOOK V—PSALMS 107-150

These emphasize the Word of God. The Messiah is pictured both in sufferings and glorious return. Closes with Hallelujah Chorus. Outstanding examples:

107 Men should praise God for His goodness

110 The Messiah as King and Priest. No Old Testament portion more frequently quoted in New Testament than this (Matt. 22:44; I Cor. 15:25; Heb. 1:3, 13; 5:6, 10; 7:17, 21)

118 The Messiah exalted (Matt. 21:42; Acts 4:11; I Peter 3:4, 7)

119 The wonderful Word of God. Only two verses, 122 and 132, do not contain some reference to God's Word.

121 Jehovah the pilgrim's help

133 The beauty of brotherly unity

137 Grief of the exiles

150 Universal praise

NOTE ON THE IMPRECATORY PSALMS: About 20 psalms contain prayers for the overthrow and defeat of the wicked (principal ones—7, 35, 69, 109). Some have thought these curses unseemly on the lips of God's children and their inclusion in God's Word as requiring some apology. They need some explanation but no apology:

1. The Holy Spirit, who inspired the Psalms, has the right to condemn sin and sinner.

2. These curses are in accordance with the law—"an eye for an eye and a tooth for a tooth" (Ps. 28:4).

3. These curses are in harmony with the teachings of our Lord and His apostles (see e.g., Matt. 18:6; 23; Gal. 1:8, 9; James 5:3; II Peter 2:12, 22; Jude 12, 15, and many other such passages).

4. These curses are not upon those whom the psalmist personally dislikes, but on those who oppose him because they oppose God and His cause.

5. Some of these curses have reference to prophecies of Scripture, and rather express what would be, than what the author wished to be (cf. Ps. 137:8, 9 with Isa. 13:16; Jer. 50:15; 51:6, 56).

6. Some of these curses have to do prophetically with the betrayal of Christ (Ps. 40; 55; 69; 109).

7. God's grace and mercy are revealed in His repeated warnings to the wicked (Ps. 2:12)

PROVERBS

Introduction

I. AUTHOR

Most of book, at least, was written by Solomon

(1:1; 10:1; 25:1; cf. II Chron. 1:10; Eccl. 12:9; I Kings 4:32). Agur (30:1)—"collector," and Lemuel (31:1)—"devoted to God" may be other names for Solomon himself. If not, we know nothing else of these writers.

II. RECIPIENTS

The writer's son (1:8; 2:1, etc.), presumably Rehoboam. The same teaching would apply to all children (4:1), and in a broader sense to mankind in general (8:1-5).

III. DATE

Written by Solomon (about 950 B.C.), but not completed until the time of Hezekiah (about 725 B.C.; see 25:1).

IV. PURPOSE OF BOOK

Contains no prophecy and little doctrine, but is rather the application of the divine wisdom to the various aspects of the daily life in this evil world. It warns against such things as bad company, impurity, intemperance, quarreling, lying, trickery in business, taking of bribes. It condemns idleness, slothfulness, pride, and avarice. It commends liberality to those in need. It teaches the fear of the Lord, obedience of children to parents, duty of parents to properly train their children, the influence of good women. Contains special instruction for the young man just going out into the world. "What the psalms are to the devotional life, the proverbs are to the practical life" (A. T. Pierson).

V. THEME
    "Laws from heaven for life on earth."
VI. KEY VERSE: 9:10
    KEY WORDS *My son*   -   -   22 times

Wise	-	-	62 times
Wisdom	-	-	54 times
Wisely	-	-	3 times
			119 times
Instruction		-	24 times
Instruct	-	-	2 times
			26 times

Knowledge - the possession of facts

Wisdom - "The ability to judge soundly and deal sagaciously with facts, especially as they relate to life and conduct" (Webster's Dictionary).

Outline of Proverbs

I. WISDOM AND FOLLY CONTRASTED (Chs. 1-9)
    (This section not in proverb form. "My son" used 15 times.)
    Ch. 1 Warning to beware of the temptation of sinners and to heed true wisdom
    Ch. 2 Warning against the evil man and the strange woman
    Ch. 3 Encouragement to trust in the Lord and to seek wisdom

Ch. 4 The importance of wisdom

Ch. 5 Warning against sexual sins

Ch. 6 Warning against suretyship, laziness and adultery

Ch. 7 The foolish youth snared by the wicked woman

Ch. 8 Wisdom exalted

Ch. 9 Wisdom contrasted with the foolish woman

II. PROVERBS OF SOLOMON PREPARED BY HIMSELF (Chs. 10-24)

Varied subjects. Chapters 10-15 provide contrasts ("antithetic")—note the use of "but." Each verse is a separate proverb. Chapters 16-24 are largely synonymous proverbs; up to 22:16 one verse is used to a proverb, from there on two or more.

III. PROVERBS OF SOLOMON COPIED OUT BY THE MEN OF HEZEKIAH (Chs. 25-29). Most of these are the one verse type ("couplet").

IV. THE WISDOM OF AGUR (Ch. 30)

V. THE WISDOM OF KING LEMUEL (Ch. 31)

ECCLESIASTES

Introduction

I. AUTHOR

Solomon (1:1, 12, 16; 2:4-11)

II. RECIPIENTS

Not specifically stated. "Young man" mentioned in 11:9 and "my son" in 12:12.

III. DATE

About 935 B.C. Probably written in Solomon's old age.

IV. PURPOSE OF BOOK

The author, in a position to fully satisfy every whim, observes and tries out various things in life to attempt by human wisdom to search out that which is good. His conclusion: 1:2; 12:13-14. The book clearly shows that even from the position of the natural man ("under the sun"), the things of this world in themselves do not bring true happiness or satisfy the human heart. Remember that this is a book of *human* wisdom (1:13), so all its statements are not necessarily true (see 2:24; 3:19-22; 7:16; 9:2). (Note—Inspiration does not mean every statement in the Bible is true, but that the *record* of it is true; for example, Satan's words.)

V. THEME

The vanity of life under the sun. (Note—*Vanity* here means not "foolish pride" but rather "emptiness" or "futility.")

VI. KEY VERSES: 1:12-14; 2:11

KEY WORDS:

Wisdom—28 times (In Proverbs, wisdom means wisdom of God "above the sun," in Ecclesiastes it means human wisdom "under the sun." According to Dr. Gray, in Proverbs it means *piety*, in Ecclesiastes *science*).

Wise - 21 times
───

Total ....49 times
    Vanity - 37 times
    Under the sun - 31 times

Outline of Ecclesiastes

I.   INTRODUCTION (1:1-11)
II.   EXPERIMENTATION (1:12-2:26)
III. OBSERVATION (3:1-8:15)
IV.   CONSIDERATION (8:16-12:7)
V.   FINAL CONCLUSION (12:8-14)

SONG OF SOLOMON
Introduction

I. AUTHOR

Solomon (1:1) . See also I Kings 4:32—this is the chief of his 1005 songs. Also called Canticles from the Latin.

II. RECIPIENTS

Not specifically stated.

III. DATE

About 970 B.C. Evidently in Solomon's early reign.

IV. PURPOSE OF BOOK

1. To glorify marriage and wedded love. Literal application

Speaks of the blissful love of Solomon and his bride (4:7, 10; 5:10, 16) .

2. To represent love of Jehovah for Israel (cf. Hos. 2:19, 20).
   Recognized by Jewish students from early times.
3. To represent love of Christ and the Church. Recognized by Christians from the beginning (see Ps. 45:6, 11; II Cor. 11:2; Eph. 5:25-33; Rev. 19:7-9; etc.).

V. THEME
   The tender love of the Bridegroom and the Bride
VI. KEY VERSE: 2:16
   KEY WORD: *Beloved*—32 times. (Usually used of the Bridegroom by the Bride.)

Outline of Song of Solomon

Heinrich Ewald, a German higher critic (1826), suggested that the story concerns a shepherdess whom Solomon tries to win away from her shepherd lover but fails. He takes her to his palace, but when she remains true to her shepherd, at last sets her free. Ironside rejects this theory for the following reasons:

1. We would hardly expect the "father of higher criticism" to open up for the first time a book of deep spiritual truth.
2. Solomon would by this theory be the villain of the story. But in the Bible he is a type of Christ (Matt. 12:42). "Solomon" means "peace."
3. Many beautiful passages which Christians through the centuries have thought to be descriptive of divine love would become mere en-

ticements of carnal desire used by Solomon in an attempt to win the shepherdess away from her true love.

Dr. Ironside presents the following as the true setting and story:

1. King Solomon had a vineyard in the hill country of Ephraim, about 50 miles north of Jerusalem (8:11).

2. He let it out to keepers (8:11). The father was apparently dead; there was a mother and two sons (1:6), also two daughters, the Shulamite (6:13) and a little sister (8:8).

3. The Shulamite was the Cinderella of the family (1:5) naturally beautiful but unnoticed. Possibly her brothers were half-brothers (1:6). They made her work very hard (1:6). They denied her any privileges whatsoever, and made her keep the vineyards (1:6). She had no opportunity to care for her personal appearance (1:6). She pruned the vines (2:15) and set traps for the little foxes (2:15) She also kept the flocks (1:8). Being out in the open so much, she became very sun-burned (1:5). One day a tall handsome stranger came to the vineyard. It was Solomon disguised. He showed an interest in her, and she became embarrassed concerning her personal appearance (1:6). She takes him for a shepherd and asks about his flocks (1:7). He answers evasively (1:8), but

also speaks loving words to her (1:8, 9, 10) and promises rich gifts for the future (1:11). He wins her heart and leaves with the promise that some day he will return. She dreams of him at night and sometimes thinks he is near (3:1). Finally he does return in all his kingly splendor to make her his bride (3:6-7). A picture of Christ, who comes first as Shepherd and wins His Bride; later He will return as King, and then will be consummated the marriage of the Lamb.

I. THE BRIDE IN THE BRIDEGROOM'S PALACE REJOICES IN HIS LOVE AND MEDITATES ON THEIR FIRST MEETING AND SEPARATION (1:1-3:5)

II. THE BRIDE SEES THE BRIDEGROOM COMING IN HIS GLORY AND RESPONDS TO HIS INVITATION TO ACCOMPANY HIM (3:6-4:16).

III. THE BRIDE SLEEPS AND IS SEPARATED FROM THE BRIDEGROOM FOR A TIME BUT AT LAST FINDS HIM (5:1-6:3)

IV. THEY EXPRESS THEIR TENDER LOVE FOR EACH OTHER (6:4-8:14)

The Prophetic Books

Introduction

I. THE PROPHET

1. Contrast prophet and priest. A prophet speaks for God; not his own message or thought, but God's Word. (Note Jer. 23:16; Ezek. 13:2; Amos 3:8; Jer. 20:9; Ezek. 3, especially vv. 4, 10).

2. Old Testament names used: "man of God" (I Kings 13:1); "seer" (I Sam. 9:9; Isa. 2:1); and finally *prophet*.

3. Primary purpose of Old Testament prophet was to warn and seek for reformation. He was a patriot—note Elijah. This naturally led to prediction.

II. THE HISTORY OF PROPHECY IN THE OLD TESTAMENT

1. First specified as a prophet was Enoch (Jude 14, 15).

2. Second was Abraham (Gen. 20:7; Ps. 105:15; I Chron. 16:8-22).

3. Moses had a unique position as the appointed leader of God's people. He was a "man of God" (Josh. 14:6) and a prophet (Deut. 18:15-19).

4. During the period of the Judges—under Samuel we find a "school," sometimes called "the sons of the prophets" (I Sam. 19:18-20).

5. During the period of the Kingdom—in the matter of heroic deeds Elijah seems to be outstanding in this period, but more details are given of Elisha's ministry (see II Kings 4:1, 16; 5:26; 6:8; 7:1; 8:10; 9:6; 13:19).

The authority of the prophet was superior even to that of the king (note II Sam. 12; I Kings 11:29ff). The prophets' written messages were not all they spoke, but rather a small portion of the oral prophecies (Isa. 8:1, 16; 30:8; Jer. 30:2; 36:1-4; Hab. 2:2).

III. THE PROPHETIC BOOKS
  1. Classification
    a. Prophets before the exile
      (1) To Nineveh: Jonah, Nahum
      (2) To the ten tribes (Israel): Amos, Hosea
      (3) To Judah: Joel, Isaiah, Zephaniah, Jeremiah, Habakkuk
      (4) To both Israel and Judah: Micah
    b. Prophets of the exile—Daniel, Ezekiel, Obadiah (against Edom)
    c. Prophets after the exile—Haggai, Zechariah, Malachi
  2. Future periods of time prophetically referred to
    a. Immediate future (Isa. 38:5, 6)
    b. Period of the northern kingdom's captivity (Amos 3:12-15)
    c. Period of the southern kingdom's captivity (Jer. 25:9-11)

    d. Time when Israel's and Judah's captors
       would be destroyed: Assyria (Nah. 3:5-7);
       Babylon (Jer. 25:12-14)

    e. First restoration of the Jew (Jer. 29:10-14)

    f. First coming of Christ (Isa. 53:1-10)

    g. Present Church Age—no *specific* prophecy
       (see Joel 2:28, 29)

    h. Tribulation Period at the close of this age
       (Dan. 9:27)

    i. Final restoration of all Israel (Ezek. 37:21, 22)

    j. Second coming of Christ (Zech. 14:1-4)

    k. The Millennium (Isa. 11:6-10)

    l. New heavens and new earth—very little (Isa. 66:22)

3. Status of these prophecies now

    a. Much already fulfilled (Isa. 7:14; Mic. 5:2, etc.)

    b. Very little now in process of fulfillment (Isa. 42:6, 7; Hos. 3:4; Dan. 9:26b (literal)

    c. Much yet to be fulfilled (Isa. 2:1-5; etc.)

ISAIAH

Introduction

I. AUTHOR

Isaiah, whose name means "the salvation of Jehovah." His father's name was *Amoz* ("strong") — do not confuse with *Amos.*

Isaiah is referred to 13 times in II Kings 19, 20

(II Kings 18-20 covers about the same ground as Isa. 37-39). In II Chronicles 26:22 we are told he wrote a history of Uzziah's life, while II Chronicles 32:32 mentions a history of Hezekiah. We do not now have either of these two books, except possibly a part of the latter. Isaiah is also mentioned in II Chronicles 32:20 with regard to the history of this period.

His wife evidently had the prophetic gift too (Isa. 8:3). He had two sons, who were given symbolic names, as in the case of Hosea's children (7:3; 8:4). It is thought that he ministered for a long time, possibly 60 years. There is no record of his death in the Bible, but according to Jewish tradition he was martyred during the wicked Manasseh's reign (Hezekiah's son), by being "sawn asunder" with a wooden saw. It may be he is referred to in Hebrews 11:37.

His book is quoted 80 times in the New Testament, and he is called by name 21 times in the New Testament (see Matt. 13:14; Acts 8:28).

II. RECIPIENTS

Judah and Jerusalem (1:1; 2:1; 3:1, etc.) (Incidentally there are words of warning to the northern kingdom (28:1), and to various Gentile nations: Babylon, Moab, Damascus, etc.)

III. DATE

Isaiah began prophesying during the closing days of Uzziah's reign, and through the reigns of Jotham,

Ahaz and most (at least) of Hezekiah's (1:1). Thus the dates of ministry would be 740-700 B.C. at least, possibly longer.

IV. PURPOSE OF THE BOOK

The reigns of Uzziah, Jotham and Hezekiah were good, at least superficially. That of Ahaz was extremely wicked, during which for 16 years the people were led into the worst excesses of idolatry. Many of Isaiah's prophecies of doom were given during this period. His purpose is to show that even though Judah has a "form of godliness," yet it is corrupt morally, religiously, and politically (1:4, 13, 15). He appeals to them to turn back to God or be driven from the land (1:19, 20; 6:9-12). But even though the Jews are dispersed, yet the nation has a glorious future ahead, a future wrapped up in their coming Messiah. Blessing will also come to the Gentiles. Isaiah speaks more of the Messiah than any other prophet.

V. THEME

The Justice and Grace of God

VI. KEY VERSES: 61:1-3

KEY WORDS: *The Holy One of Israel*—25 times

Judgment (or *judge*)—52 times

Comfort (or *comfortably*)—18 times

Outline of Isaiah

I. PROPHECIES OF PUNISHMENT (Chs. 1-35)

These prophecies largely concern conditions in Isaiah's day and look toward the captivity.

Ch. 1 A vision of judgment. The Lord's indictment against Judah. If they refuse to return to the Lord, they will be delivered to
the enemy

Ch. 2 A vision of future blessing for Israel, but
of judgment to precede the blessing

Ch. 3 Terrible judgments to come upon Judah
and Jerusalem

Ch. 4 The glorious kingdom that will come
after the judgments

Ch. 5 Parable of the vineyard

Ch. 6 Isaiah receives a wonderful vision of the
Lord and is given a commission

Ch. 7 The distress of King Ahaz and the sign
given to him of Immanuel; an Assyrian
invasion predicted

Ch. 8 Further information about the Assyrian
invasion

Ch. 9 The coming divine Child who will bring
peace

Ch. 10 The Assyrians, used by God to chasten
the Jews, shall be judged themselves

Ch. 11 The King and the kingdom. A further
revelation concerning the divine Child
(7:14; 9:6, 7) and of His wonderful kingdom which shall be established upon
earth

Ch. 12 The praise of Israel for kingdom blessings. During the time just referred to,
Israel shall give forth this song of praise

Chs. 13, 14 The burden of Babylon. (Burden—
a heavy message of judgment.)   Note also
statement about Lucifer (14:12-17) and
judgment on Philistia (14:31, 32)

Chs. 15, 16 The burden of Moab

Ch. 17 The burden of Damascus

Ch. 18 Appeal to the land "beyond the rivers of
Ethiopia" with regard to the final regathering of Israel

Chs. 19, 20 The burden of Egypt (and in ch. 20
Ethiopia is included) The disintegration
and decline of Egypt is pictured, but provision is made for final blessing

Ch. 21 Three more burdens: conquest of Babylon
by Media-Persia (vv. 1-10) ; conquest of
Dumah (southern district of Edom; Seir,
the chief mountain) (vv. 11, 12) ; burden of Arabia (vv. 13-16)

Ch. 22 Burden of the valley of vision—refers to
Jerusalem itself and its lack of repentance
even in face of Assyrian army. Last part
of chapter contains a curse upon Shebna,
the unfaithful treasurer of the house of
David; and a blessing upon Eliakim who
succeeds him

Ch. 23 The burden of Tyre. Refers to Babylonian conquest. Tyre, like Israel, shall be
restored in 70 years; but Tyre does not
turn to the Lord then. However, there

will come a day when she does turn to
Him (v. 18)

Ch. 24 God's wrath to be poured out upon the
earth before the kingdom age. (Compare the judgments of Revelation.)

Ch. 25 A song of praise to Jehovah for the wonderful things He will do

Ch. 26 The worship and testimony of the Jews
in the day of the future restoration. (We
can testify to this now.)

Ch. 27 Further statement as to the judgment of
their enemies and the restoration of the
Israelites

Ch. 28 (The prophet now turns from the distant
future to the near future.)
Woe to Ephraim and warning to the rulers
of Jerusalem

Ch. 29 Woe to Ariel, but with a promise of deliverance and future blessing

Chs. 30, 31 Woe to the rebellious children that
go down to Egypt for help. Judah seeks
help from Egypt when they should be
seeking it from the Lord. But again a
promise of deliverance from the Assyrians

Ch. 32 The coming King; His righteous government and the blessing of the Israelites

Ch. 33 Woe to Assyria, the treacherous spoiler

Ch. 34 Judgment on all the nations. Looks forward to the tribulation period of the last
days

Ch. 35 The blessing of Israel in the kingdom age.
(After speaking of the judgment on the
nations in the day of the Lord, ch. 34, the
prophet now turns to the blessing of redeemed Israel in the glorious kingdom to
be established afterward.)

II. PARENTHETICAL HISTORICAL SECTION (Chs. 36-
39)

This section indicates the conclusion of the Assyrian power and the beginning of the Babylonian.

Ch. 36 Jerusalem besieged by Sennacherib's army
Ch. 37 Jerusalem delivered by the Lord
Ch. 38 Hezekiah's illness and recovery
Ch. 39 Hezekiah's proud display to the heathen
Babylonian ambassadors and the prophecy
of Babylonian conquest

III. PROPHECIES OF BLESSING (Chs. 40-66)

This section, generally speaking, prophesies blessing for Israel, beginning with the return from the
Babylonian exile and looking forward to the supreme
blessing under the Messiah.

Ch. 40 The Comfort of God for Israel
Outline: 1. The Voice of God (vv. 1, 2)
Command to comfort God's people
2. The Voice of the Forerunner (vv.
3-5)
Preparing for the Christ
3. The Unnamed Voice (vv. 6-8)
Man's frailty and the abiding Word

4. The Voice of the Prophet (vv. 9-30)
   a. The message of the Saviour God
      (vv. 9-11)
   b. The message of the Creator God
      (vv. 12-20)
   c. The message of the Sustaining
      God (vv. 21-26)
   d. The Message of the Empower-
      ing God (vv. 27-31)

Ch. 41 God overrules in the kingdoms, but men.
refuse to see His hand at work, turning
instead to idols. The nation Israel pictured as God's servant and therefore not
to fear

Ch. 42 Jehovah's ideal servant. (Note three servants of Jehovah in Isaiah—see note in
Scofield Bible, page 749.)

Ch. 43 Israel redeemed and restored. Looks beyond the return from the Babylonian captivity to the final restoration of Israel that
is yet future

Ch. 44 Israel called on to trust in God their Redeemer and shown the folly of idolatry

Ch. 45 The greatness of God. In contrast to
idols, who know nothing, God can fore-
tell the future; the proof—Cyrus named
long before his birth (44:28; 45:1)

Ch. 46 The power of the Lord and the impotence
of idols

Ch. 47 The destruction of Babylon. (Remember that this, as other prophecies in Isaiah, was written even before Babylon came to full power.)

Ch. 48 The deliverance of Israel from Babylon

Ch. 49 The salvation to be brought to the ends of the earth by Jehovah's Servant the Messiah. (Note—this individual servant distinguished from the nation in vv. 5, 6.)

Ch. 50 Israel's rejection of the Messiah predicted; His steadfastness in the face of suffering

Ch. 51 The future redemption and restoration of Israel

Ch. 52 Zion delivered by Jehovah's salvation

Ch. 53 The substitutionary sacrifice of the suffering Saviour. (52:13-15 really a part of this message.) "The gem of Old Testament prophecy"

Ch. 54 The joy and blessedness of redeemed Israel

Ch. 55 The invitation to appropriate God's salvation

Ch. 56 A call to righteousness in view of the coming salvation

Ch. 57 Even in troublous times the righteous will be blessed and the wicked will have no peace

Ch. 58 A call to repentance—the Israelites shown that empty formalities of religion will not satisfy the Lord

Ch. 59 Israel's sin keeps them from the Lord; a Redeemer to come to Zion (second coming of Christ in view here—see Rom. 11:26, 27)

Ch. 60 The glory of Israel restored. The glorious change that shall come to Zion during the Millennium is pictured in this chapter. This change is brought about by the coming of the Redeemer (59:20)

Ch. 61 The Messiah's ministry and its result: kingdom blessing

Ch. 62 The future glory of Jerusalem

Ch. 63 Vengeance on Edom and blessing to Israel

Ch. 64 An appeal to Jehovah for forgiveness for Israel

Ch. 65 Because of their sinfulness, Jehovah will pass by Israel to give blessing to the Gentiles; but Israel will be gloriously restored

Ch. 66 A final picture of Israel's millennial blessing

JEREMIAH

Introduction

I. AUTHOR

Jeremiah the prophet (Dan. 9:2; Matt. 2:17). Meaning of the name Jeremiah is uncertain. He was from a priestly family in Anathoth (see Jer. 1:1; cf. I Kings 2:26). His father was named Hilkiah (1: 1). Received divine call while still quite young (1:6—

note "child" here translated "young man" in II Sam. 18:5). Probably under 25 when call came. Apparently he lived at first in Anathoth (three miles north of Jerusalem), and came to the city to bring his prophecies; but when the townspeople and even his own kinsman plotted against his life, he moved to Jerusalem (11:21; 12:6). He remained unmarried at the command of the Lord (16:1-2).

Jeremiah was very unpopular with the people, because he predicted that Jerusalem would fall to the Babylonians, and advised surrender to Nebuchadnezzar. He endured a great deal of persecution until the final overthrow by Nebuchadnezzar (18:18; 37:15; 38; 40:1). At that time he was offered protection and a home in Babylon, but he refused to leave his country. He stayed with the remnant until Gedaliah, the governor appointed by Nebuchadnezzar, was murdered. Against his advice, the remnant, under Johanan, then fled to Egypt, forcing him to go along. His final prophecies were from that land (chs. 43-44). Tradition states that he died in Egypt, and according to one account was stoned there.

II. RECIPIENTS

The main body of the book (chs. 2-45) to Judah and Jerusalem (2:2; 4:3; 6:1; 7:1, etc.). (Northern kingdom already carried into captivity.)

Also Jeremiah is called "a prophet unto the nations" (1:5). His fulfilling of this ministry is

shown in chapters 46-51, where he prophesies against
10 other nations.

III. DATE OF WRITING

Jeremiah began to prophesy during the thirteenth
year of the good king Josiah's reign (1:2) and continued to the end of the reign of Zedekiah, the last
king (1:3), and also somewhat beyond this time in
Egypt. Thus he prophesied slightly more than 40
years during the reign of these kings, plus the time
after Zedekiah's downfall. (This may have been 26
more years, judging by the last date in the book—
52:31). This would be from about 626-586 B.C.
and probably to 560 B.C.

IV. PURPOSE OF BOOK

Jeremiah began to prophesy during the reign of
a good king (Josiah), during whose administration
the temple was repaired and idol worship put down
(II Chron. 34). Jeremiah saw that this reform was
very superficial, however, and that Judah was following hard after the way that had brought destruction to Israel (3:6-10).

During the reign of the following kings the
progress was ever and openly downward. So Jeremiah
is commissioned to bring the last appeal from Jehovah before destruction (7:2-7). He is to announce the inevitable doom that is coming upon
Jerusalem and Judah (7:13-16), and that at the hand
of Nebuchadnezzar and Babylon (21:1-10). The
sad message he had to bring caused him great per-

sonal suffering (see 9:1; also Lamentations), so that he is called the "weeping prophet." He also had a message of judgment on the nations round about. But there is a brighter side to his message. He alone sets the Babylonian captivity at 70 years (25:11; 29:10) and he also tells of a wonderful new covenant (31:31-34).

V. THEME

The Sinfulness of Judah Brings About the Babylonian Captivity

VI. KEY VERSES: 21:7, 14

KEY WORDS: *Iniquity* (with *sin, sinned, transgress* and *transgression*) —53 times

Captive (with *captivity*) —51 times

Scatter—14 times

Evil—81 times (refers to evil the people did and also to the evil God would do to them)

Outline of Jeremiah

I. THE CALL AND EMPOWERING OF THE PROPHET (Ch. 1)

II. JUDAH CONDEMNED AND THE BABYLONIAN CAPTIVITY PREDICTED (Chs. 2-29)

Ch. 2 The nation condemned for forsaking the Lord and serving other gods

Ch. 3 Judah failed to take the downfall of Israel to heart; when Israel repents and turns back to the Lord a future day of blessing is promised

terrible judgment soon to come; but with
the threat of dispersion is a promise of
future restoration

Ch. 17 Not God's law but Judah's sin is engraved
upon their heart; God will reward them
according to their deeds

Their sin of profaning the Sabbath especially mentioned

Ch. 18 The potter and his clay used as the basis
of an appeal to the men of Judah to turn
back to God, but they refuse

Ch. 19 The broken bottle used as a sign of the
destruction to come on Judah and Jerusalem

Ch. 20 Jeremiah placed in the stocks by Pashur;
his complaint to the Lord

Ch. 21 Jeremiah's message to Zedekiah the last
king of Judah: the city will be given into
Nebuchadnezzar's hand

Ch. 22 A warning message to King Jehoiakim.
This chapter goes back in time to a point
somewhat before chapter 21

Note briefly the history of the last five
kings of Judah: After good King *Josiah's*
(1) death, his son *Jehoahaz* (2) (Shal-
lum of v. 11) became king, but reigned
only three months before being carried
into captivity into Egypt. His wicked
brother *Jehoiakim* (3) then became king

and reigned 11 years (v. 18). Then his (Jehoiakim's) son *Jehoiachin* (4) (Coniah of v. 24) reigned a little more than three months and was carried by Nebuchadnezzar to Babylon. A third son of Josiah, *Zedekiah* (5) (ch. 21), then reigned for 11 years before the final destruction of Jerusalem.

Ch. 23 An indictment of the leaders of Israel—kings, prophets, and priests—together with a promise of future restoration and blessing under the Messiah

Ch. 24 The sign of the two baskets of figs

Ch. 25 The captivity to last 70 years; after that Babylon will be judged. Jeremiah to give the cup of God's fury to the nations; this prophecy looks beyond the Babylonian conquest to the final Day of the Lord

Ch. 26 The priests and false prophets attempt to kill Jeremiah, but he is saved by the princes and people

Ch. 27 The sign of the bonds and yokes

Ch. 28 A false prophet is rebuked

Ch. 29 A message to the first group deported to Babylon

III. RESTORATION PROMISED (Chs. 30-33)

Ch. 30 Israel to be restored after the "time of Jacob's trouble" (the Great Tribulation)

Ch. 31 Israel to be blessed under a new covenant

Ch. 32 The sign of the purchase of Hanameel's field

Ch. 33 Israel and Judah to be restored under Messiah's reign

IV. THE PROPHESIED JUDGMENT INFLICTED (Chs. 34-44)

Ch. 34 Zedekiah tries to strengthen morale by a degree of liberty, but it is a failure

Ch. 35 The obedience of the Rechabites to their ancestor puts disobedient Judah to shame

Ch. 36 Jehoiakim scorns Jeremiah's warning

Ch. 37 Jeremiah thrown in the dungeon by the princes, but later relieved by Zedekiah

Ch. 38 Jeremiah thrown into a miry dungeon, but relieved by Ebed-melech, the Ethiopian

Ch. 39 Jeremiah delivered by the Babylonians in the final overthrow of Jerusalem

Ch. 40 The remnant gathers around Governor Gedaliah after the destruction of Jerusalem

Ch. 41 Ishmael murders Gedaliah, but is put to flight by Johanan

Ch. 42 The remnant asks Jeremiah for the Lord's direction as to whether to remain in the land or flee to Egypt; they are told to remain in the land

Ch. 43 The remnant rejects God's word and flees to Egypt, taking Jeremiah

Ch. 44 Jeremiah rebukes the Jews in Egypt for their idolatry

V. PROPHECIES AGAINST THE GENTILES (Chs. 45-51)

Ch. 45 Parenthetical—A message of comfort to Baruch, Jeremiah's secretary

Ch. 46 Judgment on Egypt

Ch. 47 Judgment on the Philistines

Ch. 48 Judgment on Moab

Ch. 49 Judgment on Ammon, Edom, Damascus, Kedar, and Elam (Persia)

Ch. 50 Judgment on Babylon, at which time there will be a restoration of the Jews

Ch. 51 Further information about the judgment of Babylon. (Fulfilled by the Medes and Persians, but probably foreshadows the yet future destruction of "Babylon the Great"—Rev. 17 and 18)

VI. APPENDIX (Ch. 52)

Summary of the captivity of Judah. Begins with Zedckiah's reign and goes to a point 26 years after the destruction of Jerusalem.

LAMENTATIONS

Introduction

I. AUTHOR

The name of the author is not given in the book itself, but very strong traditions, dating back to the third century B.C., ascribe the book to Jeremiah. The Septuagint begins the book with this statement (not found in the Hebrew Old Testament): "It came to pass that, after Israel was taken captive and Jerusalem was made desolate, Jeremiah sat weeping, and lamented with this lamentation over Jerusalem, and said. . . ."

The book was evidently written by an eyewitness of the destruction of Jerusalem by the Babylonians, which Jeremiah certainly was. Internally there are similarities between this little book and the prophecy of Jeremiah, so undoubtedly he was the human author of Lamentations.

II. RECIPIENTS

Judah and Jerusalem—2:13; 3:40-41, etc.

Edom—4:21-22

All who observe the destruction of Jerusalem—1:12

The Lord—1:20; 2:20, etc.

III. DATE OF WRITING

About 586 B.C.

IV. PURPOSE OF BOOK

To express the sorrow in the heart of the prophet over the destruction of Jerusalem—a destruction brought about because of the sin and rebellion of God's people. In this way we are given at least a faint understanding of the sorrow in the heart of God when He is forced to chasten His people. The New Testament teaching in Hebrews 12:5-6, 11 is aptly illustrated in this book, and an example is given to the Jews of the proper way to be "exercised" by the chastening of the Lord.

V. Theme

A Lament Over the Desolation of Jerusalem

VI. Key Verse: 1:1

Key Words: *Zion*—15 times (speaks of Jerusalem as the spiritual center of the land)

Jerusalem—7 times

Desolate—7 times

Outline of Lamentations

I. The Affliction and Miseries of Jerusalem (Ch. 1)

II. The Destruction of Zion a Judgment from the Lord (Ch. 2)

III. The Suffering of the Prophet (Ch. 3) (Jeremiah a type of Christ who also wept over Jerusalem, Luke 19:41)

IV. The Present Desolation Contrasted with the Past Splendor (Ch. 4)

V. An Appeal to God for Mercy (Ch. 5)

EZEKIEL

Introduction

I. Author

Ezekiel ("God will strengthen"). He was, like Jeremiah, a priest (1:3). His father was Buzi. He ministered in Babylon, where he had been carried as a captive, probably along with Jehoaichin, as he dates all his prophecies from this king's captivity (1:1; cf. II Kings 24:14-15). Thus he was carried into captivity in 598 B.C., about 8 years after Daniel

had been taken to Babylon, and 12 years before
Jerusalem was finally destroyed (Ezek. 33:21) at the
time of Zedekiah's captivity. He seems to have been
25 years old when carried to Babylon, and to have
received his call at 30 (1:1-2), the age when priests
usually took up their official duties (Num. 4:1-3).

II. RECIPIENTS

The children of Israel (2:3; 3:1), especially those
already in captivity (3:11; 11:25). Also messages for
the Gentiles (e. g., 25:3; 27:3).

III. DATE OF WRITING

Ezekiel began to prophesy in the fifth year of
Jehoiachin's captivity (1:2). The last date in his
book is the twenty-seventh year (29:17). Thus he
prophesied at least 22 years (593-571 B.C.).

IV. PURPOSE OF BOOK

The opening part of the book (1-24) was written
before the final fall of Jerusalem. His fellow captives stubbornly persisted in believing Jerusalem
would never be taken nor the temple destroyed.
Ezekiel had the unpleasant task of showing them
that these judgments would take place and also why.
He was in addition appointed to show the surrounding Gentile nations their own inevitable judgment.
But after Jerusalem had fallen, Ezekiel's ministry is
climaxed by the task of revealing the future restoration of Israel and the coming glory of Jerusalem.

V. THEME

The Captivity of the Children of Israel and Their

Glorious Restoration.

VI. KEY VERSES: 36:17-19, 24-28

   KEY WORDS: *"And ye* (or *they,* or *thou,* etc.)
   shall know that I am the Lord"—70 times

   "Son of man"—91 times (This expression used
   by Christ of Himself 79 times. "As used of
   Ezekiel, the expression indicates, not what the
   prophet is in himself, but what he is to God: a
   son of man (a) chosen, (b) endued with the
   Spirit (c) sent of God. All this is true also of
   Christ, who was, furthermore, the representative man—the head of regenerate humanity"—
   Scofield.)

Outline of Ezekiel

I. JUDGMENT ON JUDAH AND JERUSALEM (Chs. 1-24)
   (Given before the fall of Jerusalem.)

   Ch. 1 Ezekiel's vision of the glory of God. "The
         key word to the vision is *likeness.* . . . It
         was a likeness, a similitude, a parable, a
         picture. He did not see what no man has
         seen, but he saw visions of Jehovah in the
         form of a likeness" (G. Campbell Mor-
         gan). "No human mind can visualize the
         description in its intricate details" (Iron-
         side)

   Ch. 2 Ezekiel is commissioned

   Ch. 3 Ezekiel eats the roll and is made a watch-
         man

Ch. 4 Three signs: tile, posture, and defiled bread

Ch. 5 Sign of the shaving of the head and beard of Ezekiel

Ch. 6 Prophecy against the mountains of Israel

Ch. 7 Prophecy against the land of Israel

(Chs. 8-11 contain visions of Jerusalem, showing the necessity for judgment)

Ch. 8 Vision of abominations in the temple

Ch. 9 Vision of the man with the inkhorn

Ch. 10 Vision of fire scattered over Jerusalem

Ch. 11 Vision of the wicked princes and the departed glory—but also a promise of restoration after judgment

Ch. 12 Sign of the prophet's removal

Ch. 13 Prophecy against the false prophets

Ch. 14 Prophecy against the idolatrous elders

Ch. 15 Parable of the fruitless vine

Ch. 16 Parable of the adulterous woman (Jerusalem)

Ch. 17 Parable of the two eagles

Ch. 18 The Lord repudiates the proverb of "sour grapes" and teaches personal responsibility

Ch. 19 Lamentation for the princes and the nation

Ch. 20 The Lord's goodness and Israel's failure
Verses 1-9   Israel's sins while still in Egypt
Verses 10-17 Israel's sins in the wilderness after leaving Egypt

Ch. 32 Lamentation for Pharaoh and Egypt

III. THE RESTORATION OF ISRAEL AND THE FUTURE GLORY OF JERUSALEM (Chs. 33-48)

Ch. 33 The fall of Jerusalem   (Also contains instructions for the captive Jews.)

Ch. 34 The regathering and restoration of Israel by their Shepherd

Ch. 35 Judgment on Idumea (Edom)

Ch. 36 Restoration and conversion of Israel

Ch. 37 The valley of dry bones and the two sticks

Ch. 38 Gog, of Magog, attacks Israel in the latter days

Ch. 39 Gog utterly defeated by divine agency

The closing visions (chs. 40-48) were given 13 years after destruction of the temple and speak of a new temple unlike any that has ever yet been built.

Ch. 40 Vision of the millennial temple

Chs. 41, 42 Specifications of the temple

Ch. 43 The glory of the Lord returns to fill the temple

Ch. 44 Regulations for the priestly service in the temple

Ch. 45 The portion of the land for the priests and prince

Ch. 46 The worship and offerings of the prince and people

Ch. 47 The healing river from the sanctuary; boundaries of the land

Ch. 48 Land divided among the 12 tribes (7 to north of Jerusalem, 5 to south); the Lord present in Jerusalem

Note: The "prince" is not Christ but a mortal man. This is established by 45:22; 46:16-18; 46:2; 45:9-11.

DANIEL
Introduction

I. AUTHOR

Daniel ("God is my judge") (7:1; 8:1; 9:2; 10:1, 2 etc.). A prophet who lived during the reigns of Nebuchadnezzar, Belshazzar, Darius, and Cyrus (approximately 618-534 B.C.). Daniel is also mentioned in Ezekiel 14:14, 20; 28:3 as both a wise and righteous man. His book is referred to a number of times in the New Testament (note especially Matt. 24:15; Mark 13:14). Daniel was among the first of the Jewish captives carried to Babylon (1:1, 3, 6). He was prominent in both the Babylonian and Persian kingdoms (see 2:48; 5:29; 6:1-3, 28).

II. RECIPIENTS

Not specifically stated. Daniel 2:4—7:28 is written in Aramaic (the language used by the Babylonians at this time, so was evidently intended to be read by them as well as by the Jews). The rest is in Hebrew, being intended especially for the consolation of Israel.

III. DATE

Events recorded in the book cover a period of

about 72 years: from third year of King Jehoiakim (1:1, 2) to third year of Cyrus (10:1), 606-534 B.C.

IV. PURPOSE OF BOOK

"The book is not intended to give an account of the life of Daniel. It gives neither his lineage, nor his age, and recounts but a few of the events of his long career. Nor is it meant to give a record of the history of Israel during the exile, nor even of the captivity in Babylon. Its purpose is to show how by His providential guidance, His miraculous interventions, His foreknowledge and almighty power, the God of heaven controls and directs the forces of nature and the history of nations, the lives of Hebrew captives and of the mightiest of the kings of the earth, for the accomplishment of His divine and beneficent plans for His servants and people" (Robert Dick Wilson, in *International Standard Bible Encyclopaedia*).

"In Daniel we have the revelation of the power and wisdom of the Lord God in the government of the world to the end of the days" (G. Campbell Morgan).

V. THEME

The Beginning, Nature, Course, and Conclusion of "the Times of the Gentiles" (Luke 21:24)

VI. KEY VERSES: 7:13-14, 17-18

KEY WORDS: *King*—183 times
Kingdom—55 times
Daniel—74 times

Outline of Daniel

I. HISTORICAL SECTION ("THE HISTORIC NIGHT") (Chs. 1-6)

Ch. 1 The king's food and the faithful Hebrew youths

Ch. 2 Nebuchadnezzar's dream of the great image

Ch. 3 The faithful Jews in the fiery furnace

Ch. 4 The humbling of Nebuchadnezzar

Ch. 5 Belshazzar and the handwriting on the wall

Ch. 6 Daniel in the lions' den

II. PROPHETICAL SECTION ("THE PROPHETIC LIGHT") (Chs. 7-12)

Ch. 7 The vision of the four beasts and the little horn

Ch. 8 The vision of the ram (Persia) and the rough goat (Greece)

Ch. 9 Daniel's prayer and the vision of the 70 weeks

Ch. 10 The vision of the glory of God

Ch. 11 Prophecies concerning Persia, Grecia, and "the time of the end"

Ch. 12 The great tribulation and the resurrection

HOSEA

Introduction

I. AUTHOR

Hosea—name means "salvation"; same as Joshua's original name (Deut. 32:44); also same name as last king of Israel (II Kings 17:1-6). His father was Beeri (1:1, "expounder"). Beyond the history of his marriage, we know nothing of Hosea personally.

II. RECIPIENTS

Primarily to Israel, the northern kingdom sometimes called Ephraim (1:1, 4-6; 4:1; 5:1, etc.) However, there is also warning from time to time to Judah, the southern kingdom (as in Amos) (4:15; 5:5, 10; 5:12-14, etc.).

III. DATE OF WRITING

During the reign of Jeroboam II (great grandson of Jehu) in Israel; and of Uzziah, Jotham, Ahaz, and Hezekiah in Judah (1:1). Between 785-725 B.C. He wrote before the Assyrian captivity of the northern kingdom, which took place during the early part of the reign of Hezekiah in Judah (721 B.C.). Contemporary with Amos (but younger) and Micah (but older) in Israel; and of Isaiah in Judah.

IV. PURPOSE OF BOOK

Spiritually speaking, Israel was Jehovah's wife. But she had been unfaithful to Him and had gone deeper and deeper into idolatry and sin from the time of Jeroboam I on. So Hosea is to announce that Jehovah is going to chasten His unfaithful "wife," but that eventually He will buy her back and restore her to the place of blessing. This is illustrated by a personal experience of Hosea.

V. THEME

Unfaithfulness, chastisement and restoration.

VI. KEY VERSES: 3:1; 2:13-16

KEY WORD: *Whoredom* (with *whoring*—twice) —14 times

"The practice of harlotry; idolatry or unfaithfulness to God" (Webster)

Outline of Hosea

I. THE UNFAITHFULNESS OF ISRAEL ILLUSTRATED BY HOSEA'S MARRIAGE (Chs. 1-3)

Ch. 1 The prophet's family relations are to be a picture of Israel's relation with Jehovah. The chapter pictures both Israel's downfall and their future restoration

Ch. 2 Israel, the disowned wife of Jehovah, is to be set aside and chastised but eventually will be restored

Ch. 3 Hosea's unfaithful wife, who had left him, is brought back again, but is kept in seclusion for "many days" before being restored to her full position as wife; a picture of Israel's condition during the present age—free from idolatry, but without a king or their ancient rites of religion—after which they are to be restored.

II. THE UNFAITHFULNESS OF ISRAEL LITERALLY DESCRIBED AND CONDEMNED (Chs. 4-13)

Chs. 4, 5 The Lord's controversy with the people, priests, and princes of Israel—there is no truth, no mercy, no knowledge of God in the land, so God has set them aside for a time

Ch. 6 They have treacherously broken their covenant with God.

Ch. 7 Woe pronounced on Israel because they have turned away from God

Ch. 8 Israel has forgotten his Maker; he has sown the wind and must reap the whirlwind

Ch. 9 Because they refused to hearken to God they shall be "wanderers among the nations."

Ch. 10 Their king shall be utterly cut off. (Fulfilled about 30 years later.)

Ch. 11 God's tender love for Israel in spite of their apostasy

Ch. 12 Their blood is on their own heads

Ch. 13 They have destroyed themselves by going deeper and deeper into sin—"Samaria shall become desolate"

III. THE PROMISE OF FUTURE BLESSING AFTER JUDGMENT (Ch. 14)

JOEL
Introduction

I. AUTHOR

Joel, the son of Pethuel (1:1). Name means "Jehovah is God." Nothing more known of Joel, as there is no other reference in the Bible except Acts 2:16 (which confirms he was a prophet).

II. RECIPIENTS

All the inhabitants of the land (1:2). Evidently refers to land of Judah, from various references such as 3:1, 17. (Israel in 3:2 has prophetic reference to all 12 tribes). Special mention made to "old men" (1:2), husbandmen and vinedressers (1:11), and priests (1:13).

III. DATE OF WRITING

Uncertain, but probably rather early, as no mention is made of Assyria or Babylon, but Tyre, Sidon, the Philistines and Egypt are pictured as Israel's chief enemies. Probably written somewhere around 838-756 B.C.

IV. PURPOSE OF BOOK

A terrible plague of devouring locusts, vividly described in chapter 1, had just taken place in the land. It is a judgment from God. The people are urged to call on the Lord and turn back to Him. However, this plague of locusts is shown to have a spiritual significance and to foreshadow a coming "day of the Lord," when the Gentiles will be judged and Israel finally blessed. Beginning with chapter 2 the literal plague of locusts is left behind and this future "day of the Lord" is in view.

V. THEME

The Day of the Lord. The present is in a sense *man's* day (I Cor. 4:3 lit.) Someday the Lord will have *His* day—not a 24-hour day, but a period of time beginning with the return of Christ and the judgments just preceding it, and extending through His millennial reign.

VI. KEY VERSES: 2:28-32

KEY WORD: *Day of the Lord*—5 times

Outline of Joel

I. THE FUTURE "DAY OF THE LORD" PREFIGURED BY THE LOCUST PLAGUE (Ch. 1)

The Plague of locusts is described (vv. 1-12)

The people are called to repentance (vv. 13, 14)

The day of the Lord foreshadowed by the insect plague (vv. 15-20)

II. EVENTS OF THE FUTURE DAY OF THE LORD (Ch. 2)

Israel in terror because of the approach of a northern army (vv. 1-10)

The Lord's army ready for the invader (v. 11)

Repentance of the people in that day (vv. 12-17)

The Lord delivers and blesses His people (vv. 18-27)

The promise of the Spirit (vv. 28-32), partly fulfilled at Pentecost and during the present age, but awaiting complete fulfillment at the time of the second advent

III. ORDER OF EVENTS IN THE DAY OF THE LORD (Ch. 3)

Regathering of Israel (v. 1)

Judgment of nations in valley of Jehoshaphat (vv. 2-15)

Kingdom blessing for Israel (vv. 17-21)

AMOS

Introduction

I. AUTHOR

Amos. Name means "burden." Until specially called by the Lord, he was a "herdman" (1:1; 7:14, 15). This may mean shepherd, as he was a cattle-man (3:12). He also describes himself as "gatherer of sycomore fruit" (7:14) —something like figs, eaten only by poorer people. He came from Tekoa, a town in Judah, six miles southeast of Bethlehem.

II. RECIPIENTS

Israel (1:1). This is the northern kingdom as he distinguishes Israel and Judah in the verse. There are a number of other references to Israel: 2:6, 11; 4:12; 5:1, 4. Cities of the northern kingdom are also mentioned a number of times: Bethel and Gilgal as centers of idolatry. But the message is to be a warning to the southern kingdom as well (3:1; 2:4, 5; 6:1).

III. DATE OF WRITING

During the reign of Uzziah in Judah and Jeroboam II in Israel (1:1), between 810 and 785 B.C. Amos was thus a contemporary with Hosea (Israel), and probably with Joel (Judah) and Jonah (Nineveh).

IV. PURPOSE OF BOOK

Amos lived in a time of material prosperity for Israel, during the reign of Jehu's great-grandson. However, the sins of Israel were many and needed the warning voice of a fearless man of God. Like the unnamed prophet many years before (I Kings 13), Amos, a man of Judah, was raised up to carry a warning to Jeroboam II, and Israel. He speaks of such sins as idolatry, luxury, revelry, debauchery, oppression, extortion, bribery, injustice. He gives a message of the sure judgment to come on Israel because of these sins. There is, however, first of all, a word concerning judgment on the Gentiles around Israel (1:1-2:3) and on Judah (2:4, 5). But after judgment is to be blessing for Israel (9:11-15).

V. THEME

The inevitable judgment of God on sin.

VI. KEY VERSES: 4:11, 12

KEY WORDS: *transgression* (and *transgress,* once)
—12 times
"I will not turn away the punishment thereof"
—8 times

Outline of Amos

I. INEVITABLE JUDGMENT ON THE NATIONS (Chs.
1, 2)
In these first two chapters judgment is pronounced
on six Gentile nations surrounding Israel; then
on Judah and Israel themselves. Note that the
last two messages follow the same form as the first
six. God is the God of the nations as well as of
the Israelites—all are responsible to Him

1. JUDGMENT ON DAMASCUS AND SYRIA (1:3-5).
The particular sins mentioned for all these
Gentile nations relate to their mistreatment
of Israel (Gen. 12:3; Num. 24:9). Syria is
charged with cruelty

2. JUDGMENT ON GAZA (1:6-8). Southernmost of
the five capital cities of the five divisions of
Philistia. Here stands for all of Philistia.
(Three of the other cities mentioned in v. 8).
Sin condemned is their slave trade

3. JUDGMENT ON TYRE, LEADING CITY OF PHOEN-
ICIA (1:9, 10). Acted as slave agent in spite
of covenant agreeing not to do so

4. JUDGMENT ON EDOM (two cities of Edom mentioned—Teman and Bozrah (1:11, 12). Im-
plicable hatred and unforgiveness.

    5. JUDGMENT ON AMMON (RABBAH THE CAPITAL)
       (1:13-15). Cruel aggression

    6. JUDGMENT ON MOAB (2:1-3). (Kirioth, chief
       city of Moab.) Reference to the sin rather
       obscure

    7. JUDGMENT ON JUDAH (2:4-5). Despised the
       law of the Lord

    8. JUDGMENT ON ISRAEL (2:6-16). They have cor-
       rupted justice and have oppressed the poor and
       needy. Impurity and idolatry also mentioned.
       They refused to heed God's prophets.

II. FULLER STATEMENT OF JUDGMENT ON ISRAEL
   (Chs. 3-6)

   Note repetition of "Hear this word" (3:1; 4:1;
   5:1)

   Ch. 3 Israel has had a special place of privilege,
        and therefore has a great responsibility.
        God will surely punish their iniquities

   Ch. 4 God has chastened Israel in various ways
        to warn them; yet they have not heeded

   Ch. 5 Lamentation over Israel because they will
        not seek the Lord and escape judgment

   Ch. 6 Those living in callous luxury, indiffer-
        ent to the claims of the Lord, shall be
        first to go into captivity

III. VISIONS OF JUDGMENT (7:1—9:10).

    1. Vision of grasshoppers (7:1-3). The interces-
       sion of Amos saves them from this

    2. Vision of fire (7:4-6)

3. Vision of the plumbline (7:8, 9). (Plumbline—a line or cord having a weight at one end, used to test verticality.) A symbol of judgment. No intercession here by Amos. Like Abraham he stops

4. Attempt to silence Amos (7:10-17). Historical section

5. Vision of summer fruit (ch. 8). Israel ripe for judgment

6. Vision of the smashed temple and prophecy of death (9:1-10)

IV. MILLENNIAL BLESSING FOR ISRAEL AFTER THE JUDGMENT (9:11-15)

"In that day," that is, after the sifting of verse 9 is complete. A reference to the Millennium yet ahead. James quotes verses 11 and 12 in Acts 15:13-18 as being God's future program *after* He accomplishes in this present age His purpose of "visting the Gentiles to take out of them a people for his name" (Acts 15:14)

OBADIAH
Introduction

I. AUTHOR

The prophet Obadiah ("worshiper of Jehovah"). About a dozen different men of this name are mentioned in the Old Testament; but apparently Obadiah 1:1 is the only reference to this particular prophet.

II. RECIPIENTS

Edom, a nation located south of the Dead Sea and descended from Esau. Edom as a nation is addressed directly throughout the prophecy.

III. DATE

Probably 586-585 B.C. This is based on the conclusion that verses 11-14 refer to the Babylonian destruction of Jerusalem by Nebuchadnezzar. Some reverent scholars disagree on this interpretation and place the date of the book considerably earlier.

IV. PURPOSE

To warn Edom of judgment soon to come upon them because of their pride and malicious treatment of Judah, in the time of Jerusalem's trouble.

V. THEME

Retribution for Edom

VI. KEY VERSE: 15

KEY WORDS: *Edom* (with Esau) —9 times
Cut off—3 times

Outline of Obadiah

I. COMPLETE DESTRUCTION OF EDOM PROPHESIED (vv. 1-9)

II. PRINCIPAL REASON FOR THIS JUDGMENT (vv. 10-16)

III. FUTURE BLESSING FOR ISRAEL AND ZION (vv. 17-21)

JONAH

Introduction

I. AUTHOR

The Prophet Jonah ("a dove"). His father was
Amittai ("truthful,") 1:1. Jonah is also mentioned
by name in II Kings 14:25, and in Matthew 12:39,
40, 41; 16:4; Luke 11:29, 30, 32. He was from
Gath-Hepher (II Kings 14:25), a city of Zebulon
(called in Joshua 19:13 "Gittah-hepher").

II. RECIPIENTS

The ministry described in the book was to the
great Gentile city of Nineveh, made by Sennacherib
the capital of Assyria. The recipients of the book
itself are not specifically stated.

III. DATE

A comparison of II Kings 14:25-27 with 13:4-7
seems to indicate that Jonah first gave the prophecy
referred to there during the reign of Jehoahaz in
Samaria. The prophecy was fulfilled during the following reigns of Joash and Jeroboam II. This means
that Jonah was contemporary in part at least, with
Elisha, who died during the reign of Joash. Jehoahaz
reigned about 820-804 B.C., so Jonah must have
ministered and have written his book somewhere
around this date.

IV. PURPOSE OF BOOK

1. To show God's love for the Gentiles as well as
   for Israel, and to illustrate His work among
   them

2. To show the Old Testament requirement for salvation for Gentiles

3. To show Israel's true purpose as exemplified in Jonah

4. To provide a typical picture of the witness of the Jewish remnant in the last days

5. To show God's method of dealing with His own disobedient servant

In form, this book is entirely different from the other prophetic books of the Old Testament. Instead of being devoted to direct prophecy, it gives instead a personal history of Jonah's dealings with God, and thus teaches its lessons in an indirect fashion. There are numerous spiritual lessons, for instance: "Trust and obey, for there's no other way to be happy in Jesus, but to trust and obey"; God's love and mercy are for *all;* God needs human servants to carry His message; God's children should obey Him first of all because of love for Him.

V. THEME

A great Gentile city repents and turns to God under the reluctant preaching of the prophet Jonah.

VI. KEY VERSE: 3:10

KEY WORD: *Prepared*—4 times

Notice the things God prepared: a wind (1:4); a tempest (1:4); a fish (1:17); a gourd (4:6); a worm (4:7), an east wind (4:8). God did not prepare a messenger, but He called a man for that purpose.

Outline of Jonah

I. JONAH DISOBEYS THE DIRECT COMMAND OF GOD
    (1:1-3)

II. JONAH BRINGS TROUBLE ON OTHERS INSTEAD OF
    BLESSING (1:4-11)

III. JONAH BRINGS THE CHASTENING HAND OF GOD
    UPON HIMSELF (1:12-2:10)
    As to the authenticity of the record of the great
    fish swallowing Jonah, see Matthew 12:40. "Some
    men are so busy with the tape-measure trying to
    find out whether a man could get inside a fish,
    they never plumb the depths of Deity"—G. Camp-
    bell Morgan

IV. JONAH'S OBEDIENCE DELIVERS THOUSANDS FROM
    DESTRUCTION (3:1-10)

V. JONAH'S OWN HEART REQUIRES FURTHER CHAST-
    ENING BECAUSE OF HIS LACK OF LOVE FOR SOULS
    4:1-11)

MICAH
Introduction

I. AUTHOR
    The prophet Micah ("who is like unto Jehovah";
the thought of his name is expressed in 7:18). He
is called the Morasthite (1:1); that is, a native of
the town of Moresheth-gath (1:14), a town about
20 miles southwest of Jerusalem. He is also mentioned as a prophet in Jeremiah 26:17-19, which
passage especially refers to him as prophesying in

the days of Hezekiah and seems to indicate that he finally died a peaceful death.

II. RECIPIENTS

Both northern and southern kingdoms—Israel and Judah (1:1, 5, etc.) .

III. DATE

Micah prophesied during the days of Jotham, Ahaz and Hezekiah (v. 1). Micah was contemporary with both Hosea and Isaiah. Thus he prophesied between 749-697 B.C.

IV. PURPOSE OF BOOK

To show the sins of the Israelites, the judgment inevitably coming because of these sins, and the eventual restoration that would finally come.

V. THEME

The judgment on all Israel because of sin, and their final restoration through God's grace.

VI. KEY VERSES: 1:5, 6, 9; 4:1-4
    KEY WORD: *Hear*—9 times
    Desolation (with *desolate*) —4 times
    Gather (with *assemble*) —9 times

Outline of Micah

I.   SIN AND JUDGMENT (Chapters 1-3)

II. GRACE AND FUTURE RESTORATION (Chaps. 4-5)

III. APPEAL AND PETITION (Chapters 6-7)

NAHUM

Introduction

I. AUTHOR

The prophet Nahum ("comforter"), who is said (1:1) to have been an Elkoshite. Elkosh is thought to have been a city of Galilee. Nahum is not mentioned in the historical books.

II. RECIPIENTS

Nineveh, the capital city of Assyria (1:1, 9; 3:5, etc.). There is also a word of encouragement for Judah (1:15).

III. DATE

The book must have been written after the destruction of No-Amon in Egypt (3:8-10). This took place 661 B.C. It was of course written before the destruction of Nineveh which came to pass in 612 B.C. Therefore the book was written sometime between 661-612 B.C.

IV. PURPOSE

About one hundred fifty years before this time Nineveh had repented under the preaching of Jonah, and had been graciously spared by the Lord. The city had again gone deep into sin, however (3:1), now the Lord through a second prophet pronounces His final condemnation—utter destruction (1:8-9). Nahum's purpose is to announce this judgment and to show the reason for it.

V. THEME
    The destruction of Nineveh.

VI. KEY VERSES: 3:5-7
    KEY WORD: *Vengeance* (with *revenge*) —3 times

Outline of Nahum

I. THE INDIGNATION OF A HOLY GOD AGAINST SIN
    SUCH AS THAT OF NINEVEH (Chap. 1)

II. PROPHECY OF THE DOOM OF NINEVEH (Chap. 2)

III. THE REASON FOR THIS DOOM (Chap. 3)

HABAKKUK
Introduction

I. AUTHOR
    The Prophet Habakkuk ("embrace") —1:1. Nothing is known of him or his life.

II. RECIPIENTS
    The book is not addressed to any particular person or group but was doubtless originally presented to Judah, just before the Babylonian conquest.

III. DATE
    No reference is made to the northern kingdom or to the Assyrians who carried the ten tribes into captivity. The Babylonian threat is pictured as imminent. So the book must have been written between the reign of Hezekiah and the time of the final overthrow of Jerusalem, possibly during the reign of Jehoiakim (610-599 B.C.).

IV. PURPOSE OF BOOK
    Somewhat like Jonah, this book does not consti-

tute a direct address to the people of Judah, but
rather relates an experience of the prophet. Habakkuk complains of God's apparent lack of concern over Judah's sin. The Lord answers that He
is concerned and will punish them by the Chaldeans.
Then the prophet complains of God's apparent lack
of concern over the cruelty of the Babylonians, and
the Lord answers that He will bring Babylon into
judgment too. Finally "at the end" (2:3) there
will come a time when "the earth shall be filled with
the knowledge of the glory of the Lord" (2:14).
The prophet closes with a psalm of absolute and
sublime trust in the Lord. Habakkuk vividly shows
the holiness and righteousness of God, who must
and will punish sin. It is also his purpose to encourage believers to wait on the Lord and trust
fully in Him regardless of outward circumstances.

V. THEME

"The just shall live by faith."

VI. KEY VERSE: 2:4

Outline of Habakkuk

I. THE PROPHET'S COMPLAINT REGARDING UN-
JUDGED SIN IN JUDAH (1:1-4)

II. THE LORD'S REPLY THAT JUDGMENT WILL
COME THROUGH THE CHALDEANS (1:5-11)

III. THE PROPHET'S COMPLAINT AGAINST THE
WICKEDNESS OF THE CHALDEANS (1:12—2:1)

IV. THE LORD'S REPLY THAT JUDGMENT WILL
COME ON THE CHALDEANS TOO (2:2-20)

V. THE PROPHET'S PRAYER FOR REVIVAL AND THE EXPRESSION OF HIS SUPREME FAITH IN THE LORD (3:1-19)

ZEPHANIAH

Introduction

I. AUTHOR

The prophet Zephaniah ("He whom Jehovah has hidden"). Zephaniah is the only one of the prophets who traces his ancestry back for several generations (1:1). He states that he is the great-great-grandson of Hezekiah (R.V.). It seems very probable that the reference is to the king of Judah by that name, and from the time of writing it would have been entirely possible for Zephaniah to have sustained such a relationship to King Hezekiah.

II. RECIPIENTS

Judah and Jerusalem (1:4). The book was written after the northern kingdom had already been carried away into captivity by Assyria. There are warnings to various Gentile nations around Israel.

III. DATE

"In the days of Josiah, the son of Amon, king of Judah" (1:1). Josiah reigned about 639-608 B.C. The book was probably written before the great reformation which was completed in the 18th year of Josiah's reign (II Chron. 34:8); that is, about 621 B.C. So 630 B.C. may be set as the approximate date of writing.

IV. PURPOSE OF BOOK
To warn Judah of the coming judgment and to comfort the faithful remnant.

V. THEME
The Day of the Lord as prefigured by the Babylonian invasion.

VI. KEY VERSES: 1:7, 12
KEY WORDS: *Day of the Lord* (with *that day, the day,* etc.) —20 times
Desolation—7 times
Remnant—4 times

Outline of Zephaniah

I. JUDGMENT ON JUDAH FORESHADOWS "THE GREAT DAY OF THE LORD" (1:1—2:3)

II. JUDGMENT ON ADJACENT NATIONS AND ON JERUSALEM FORESHADOWS THE FINAL JUDGMENT ON ALL THE NATIONS (2:4—3:8)

III. THE RESTORATION OF ISRAEL AFTER THE JUDGMENTS ARE PAST (3:9-20)

HAGGAI

Introduction-

I. AUTHOR
Haggai ("my feast"—"a name given in anticipation of the joyous return from exile"—Fausset), see 1:1, 3, 13; 2:1, etc. He was a prophet (Ezra 5:1; 6:14). According to Jewish tradition Haggai was

a Levite, who returned with Zerubbabel to Jerusalem. He died there and was buried among the priests.

II. RECIPIENTS

Especially to Zerubbabel, the governor, and to Joshua the High Priest (1:1; 2:2, 21), but also to all the people (1:13; 2:2).

III. DATE

The book covers a period of a little less than four months (1:1; 2:10, 20). This was the second year of Darius, king of Persia (called in secular history Darius Hystaspis or Darius the Great)—see 1:1; Ezra 4:24. (This is not the Darius of the Book of Daniel who lived earlier and was a Mede).

IV. PURPOSE OF BOOK

To encourage the people to rebuild the temple. Because of opposition the work had stopped for some 2 years (Ezra 4). The people had grown cold-hearted and did not make any attempt to begin the work again until exhorted by Haggai and Zechariah to do so.

V. THEME

Building the Lord's House.

VI. KEY VERSES: 1:14; 2:9.

KEY WORDS: *"the Lord's house"* (sometimes *"this house," "mine house,"* etc.)—8 times
"Consider"—5 times

Outline of Haggai

(Four messages—or five if 1:12-15 is considered a separate message)

I. **MESSAGE CONCERNING NEGLIGENCE** (1:1-15)

Date—6th month, 1st day, 2nd year of Darius—September, 520 B.C.

Excuse—"the time is not come" (v. 2)

Reproof—"consider your ways" (v. 5)

Result—obedience and godly fear (v. 12)

Work begins again 20 days later (v. 15)

II. **MESSAGE CONCERNING COURAGE** (2:1-9)

Date—7th month, 21st day—October, 520 B.C.

This temple may not be as splendid in outward adornment as the former, but it will eventually be even more glorious since the Messiah Himself shall enter it. Therefore the people are to take courage.

III. **MESSAGE CONCERNING SEPARATION** (2:10-19)

Date—9th month, 24th day—December, 520 B.C.

They had raised an altar through fear sometime before (Ezra 3:3), but one holy thing does not hallow disobedience, so God could not bless them. But now that they are separated unto Him He will bless "from this day" (v. 19).

IV. **MESSAGE CONCERNING JUDGMENT** (2:20-23)

Date—9th month, 24th day—same as III.

This message may have been an answer to a question from Zerubbabel. The nations are to be judged but Zerubbabel will be precious in God's sight when He does this great work.

ZECHARIAH

Introduction

I. AUTHOR

Zechariah (1:1, 7; 7:1, etc.) —"Jehovah remembers." He was a prophet, the son of Berechiah ("Jehovah blesses") and grandson of Iddo ("His time"). Combine the three names and the result is "Jehovah remembers and He blesses in His time"— a truth which applies to God's people of every age.

Zechariah is a common name of the Old Testament and is used of at least 27 other people. Zechariah at the time he wrote was apparently a young man (2:4). Since he wrote in the second year of Darius (1:1) and this was 18 years after the first year of Cyrus when the captive Israelites returned, he must have been a very small child when brought from Babylon. His grandfather Iddo was a priest who returned with Zerubbabel and Joshua from Babylon (Ezra 5:1; 6:14; Neh. 12:4, 16). According to tradition (Talmud) he was a member of the Great Synagogue (governing body of the Jews before the Sanhedrin) and lived to a very old age. One tradition says he met his death by martyrdom.

II. RECIPIENTS

All the people of Israel who had returned from captivity (1:2, 4; 7:5, etc.). Some messages especially addressed to Joshua the High Priest (3:8) and to Zerubbabel the governor (4:6).

III. DATE

From the second to the fourth year of King Darius (1:1; 7:1). 520-518 B.C.

IV. PURPOSE OF BOOK

Like that of Haggai, to spur the people on to complete the unfinished temple (Ezra 4:23—5:1; 6:14; Zech. 1:16; 4:8-9, etc.). Zechariah's message seems to be more in the nature of encouragement, and Haggai of rebuke. Haggai's chief task was to arouse the people to the necessity of the outward task of rebuilding the temple; whereas Zechariah goes beyond this to seek to bring about a spiritual change in the people.

Beyond all this, the Lord had future events to reveal to His people; events concerning the future of Israel, of the Gentile world powers, and especially concerning the two advents of Christ (3:8; 9:9; 14:4, etc.).

V. THEME

The two advents of the Messiah, Israel's Great Deliverer (3:8; 6:12; 9:9; 12:10; 14:3, 4).

VI. KEY VERSES: 9:9, 10

KEY WORDS: *"The Word of the Lord"* (also *"my words,"* etc.) —14 times

"The Lord of hosts"—52 times (18 times in ch. 8) ("Hosts" represents the Hebrew word *Sabaoth.*) "Implies the boundless resources at His command for His people's good"—Fausset.

Outline of Zechariah

I. THE VISIONS OF ZECHARIAH. Chs. 1-6.

"Not easy of exposition, but flaming with light, singing in hope, and resonant in confidence." (G. Campbell Morgan)

Ch. 1 INTRODUCTION (Vs. 1-6)

(After this the prophet turns to 10 prophetic visions given to him some three months later, apparently all in one night. Usual order: prophet sees something, he asks a question about it, and then is provided an interpretation.)

(1) VISION OF THE HORSES AND THE MAN AMONG THE MYRTLES (1:7-17)

Speaks of judgment on the nations because of their too severe treatment of Israel

(2) VISION OF THE FOUR HORNS (1:18-19)

Horn is a symbol of power and authority. These represent nations which have scattered Judah and Jerusalem, probably the four great powers of Daniel — Babylon, Medo-Persia, Greece and Rome

(3) VISION OF THE FOUR ARTIFICERS (1: 20-21)

These are sent of God against the world powers to conquer those who have conquered Israel. May represent

the four judgments of God (Ezek.
14:21; Rev. 6:1-8) : sword, famine,
wild animals, pestilence (Scofield)

Ch. 2 (4) VISION OF THE MAN WITH THE MEAS-
URING LINE

This "man" probably the Angel of
Jehovah (as in Ezek. 40:3 where He
measures the city again, there for millennial blessing). This vision promises blessing to Judah and Jerusalem
at that time, but doubtless looks beyond to a fuller fulfillment in the
Millennium.

Ch. 3 (5) THE VISION OF THE CLOTHING OF
JOSHUA, THE HIGH PRIEST (Ch. 3)

Joshua, the high priest, representative
of the people of Israel, appears with
filthy garments which are removed
and replaced with clean garments.
This represents what God is doing for
Israel. Secondary applications: Sets
forth a type of the sinner's filthy rags
of righteousness being exchanged for
the pure linen of the righteousness of
God through Christ. Also illustrates
the way in which Christ is the believer's advocate before the Father (I
John 2:1)

Ch. 4 (6) THE VISION OF THE CANDLESTICK AND
THE TWO OLIVE TREES (Ch. 4)

The candlestick speaks of witnessing, as do the two olive trees (v. 12) ; the oil, of the Holy Spirit, the source of true testimony. Gold speaks of divine appointment; seven is the number of completion and perfection

Ch. 5 (7) THE VISION OF THE FLYING ROLL (Ch. 5:1-4)

Speaks of judgment which must come upon Israel before full blessing can be enjoyed. Zechariah sees a wide, unfolded scroll which is in motion. The scroll contains the law; this goes through the whole land entering the houses of evildoers, upon which destruction comes to these houses. In the broad outlook this refers to judgment which must come on Israel before final millennial blessing.

(8) THE VISION OF THE WOMAN IN THE EPHAH (5:5-11)

An ephah is a measure a little larger than our bushel. The measure speaks of something having come to the full and being ready for judgment. A woman, used symbolically in Scripture, usually speaks of religious evil (see Matt. 13:33; Rev. 2:20). With a large weight of lead the wickedness is sealed within the ephah. Two other women, with wings like storks (also speaking of evil) carry the measure to Babylon (Shinar). The origin of Israel's great sin—that of idolatry—is traced to Babylon, the place where all wickedness started. Babylon too shall be judged. Probably both a local fulfillment and a future fulfillment in the destruction of spiritual Babylon (Rev. 17 and 18).

Ch. 6 (9) THE VISION OF THE FOUR CHARIOTS (Ch. 6:1-8)

Represent "the four spirits of the heavens" (v. 5) which go out to execute God's judgment on the great world powers. Both a near and a far fulfillment.

(10) THE VISION OF THE CROWNING OF JOSHUA (6:9-15).

Some consider this an actual occurrence but as the formula is the same as that used in 1:7 and 4:8 to introduce visions it seems best to class it as such. The crowning of Joshua is symbolic of the crowning of Christ, again presented as the Branch, who shall grow up and branch out according to promise from the seed of Abraham and David in the land of Israel. The temple refers not to the temple then in progress, for Zerubbabel was building that, but to the millennial temple (Ezek. 40-48). Verse 13 pictures the glorious millennial reign of Christ at which time He will be both King and Priest.

II. THE QUESTION OF BETHEL AND THE ANSWER OF JEHOVAH (Chs. 7-8)

Ch. 7 THE QUESTION OF BETHEL, AND THE BEGINNING OF JEHOVAH'S ANSWER

The book now changes to direct discourse and there is an amplification of that which has gone before. This chapter begins about two years after the visions given previously. The city of Bethel sends a deputation to speak to those considered authorities in the things of God, the prophets and priests. God had required only one fast each year, the Day of Atonement. However the Jews had added additional ones. That of the fifth month was in remembrance of the destruction of Jerusalem and the temple (II Kings 25:8; Jer. 52:12). Now since the city and temple are prospering the people wonder if there is further need for such a fast.

Jehovah's reply comes to all the people. He mentions also the fast of the seventh month, commemorating the murder of

Gedaliah by Ishmael (Jer. 41:43). He indicates that these fasts, not commanded by Him, had been carried out not as an act of true repentance but as a bare formality. There was no real sorrow for sin, so their fasting, as their feasting, was done for themselves and not unto God.

Ch. 8 THE ANSWER OF JEHOVAH (*Continued*). Jehovah's wrath is now past and there is to be blessing for Jerusalem (again a near and a far fulfillment). Fasting shall be turned into feasting (v. 19).

III. THE DOWNFALL OF THE NATIONS AND THE SALVATION OF ISRAEL (Chs. 9-14)

In this section the judgment of the nations around Israel is given and the millennial reign is pictured.

Ch. 9 THE COMING KING AND THE DELIVERANCE HE WILL BRING TO ISRAEL

Ch. 10 BLESSING FOR JUDAH AND EPHRAIM.

Ch. 11 THE TRUE SHEPHERD REJECTED FOR THE FALSE SHEPHERD

A picture of the coming of the Messiah, the True Shepherd, is given, and His rejection by Israel is foretold. This brings the wrath of God on the land and opens the way for the coming of the false shepherd, the Beast of Daniel 7:8 and Revelation 19:20, whose eventual destruction is also prophesied. Beginning in verse 7, Zechariah, representing the Good Shepherd, symbolically carries out certain actions that speak of the rejection of the Messiah. Note especially verses 12, 13

Ch. 12 The siege of Jerusalem and the deliverance by Jehovah
This chapter tells of the Battle of Armageddon, the deliverance of Jerusalem, and the kingdom blessing to follow

Ch. 13 The cleansing of Israel (vs. 1-6) and their scattering after the Shepherd is smitten (vs. 7-9)

Ch. 14 The Coming King and the Kingdom

MALACHI

Introduction

I. AUTHOR

Malachi—1:1 (name means "my messenger" or "messenger of Jehovah") . Some consider this to be not a proper name at all but rather the title of one who desires to keep himself in the background. One tradition says this is a title of Ezra but Ezra is always called a scribe and never a prophet. Though not referred to by name, Malachi is quoted a number of times in the New Testament (Matt. 11:10; 17:12; Mark 1:2; 9:11, 12; Luke 1:17; Rom. 9:13). "There is no reason to doubt that this was the real

name of a definite person." (A. C. Gaebelein).
Nothing is known of Malachi's personal life.

II. RECIPIENTS

The people of Israel who have returned to the
land after the captivity (1:1; 2:11; 3:6-7). The
priests are specially addressed (1:6; 2:1) also the
faithful group among the people (4:2, 3).

III. DATE

No date is given in the book, but evidently it was
written after the Babylonian captivity because the
people are pictured as living under a governor (1:
8), the temple worship is being carried on (1:7, 8,
10), and no idolatry is mentioned. Some think the
book was written while Nehemiah was governor,
perhaps while he was away from Jerusalem on his
visit to Shushan, others that it was written somewhat later than this because of the comparing of
1:8 with Nehemiah 5:15, 18. The date therefore
was sometime between 445 and 397 B.C.

IV. PURPOSE OF BOOK

The returned remnant was carrying on the temple
worship but had fallen into a backslidden condition.
They were insensible to the love of Jehovah (1:2)
and were not honoring God but in reality despising
His name (1:6). They were so far from the Lord
that they could not perceive their improper attitude.
This is one of the terrible features of sin—it hardens
and blinds one to his true condition. Special sins
were the worldly, careless attitude of the priests;

marriage of the people with the heathen; divorce; refusal to pay the tithes; and treacherous dealing with one another.   Haggai and Zechariah were sent to rebuke the people for failure to build the temple; Malachi reproves them for neglect of the temple and profanation of the temple worship.   This he does by the question and answer method (no less than 23 questions in the book).

V.   THEME

God's people rebuked for neglecting and profaning the worship of the Lord.

VI. KEY VERSES: 3:9-10

KEY WORDS: *Ye say*—11 times

Wherein—6 times

Cursed—7 times

Outline of Malachi

I.   THE SINS OF THE PRIESTS (1:1—2:9)

II.   THE SINS OF THE PEOPLE (2:10—3:15)

III.   THE FAITHFUL FEW (3:16—4:6)

Introduction to the New Testament and to the Four Gospels

I. THE PLACE OF THE NEW TESTAMENT
  1. Reasons for its being written
     a. To complete the incomplete revelation of the Old Testament (Heb. 1:1, 2; Jer. 31: 31-34; Mal. 3:1).
     b. To show the fulfillment of the Old Testament prophecies (Luke 4:21; John 13:18; 17:12; Acts 1:16, and many other references). The Old Testament pointed to the coming Messiah; the New Testament shows the fulfillment of that hope.
     c. To present in its fullness the way of salvation (John 20:31).
     d. To give all needed revelation for God's children (John 4:25; 17:8; 16:12-13). This especially concerns the Church (Matt. 16:18; Eph. 5:23-32).

  2. Distinguishing characteristic
     Grace (John 1:17)

159

3. Divisions
   a. History—4 Gospels and Acts.............. 5 books
   b. Doctrine—Epistles ....21 books
      (14 by Paul)
   c. Prophecy—Revelation .... 1 book
                                                    —
                                                  27 books

II. THE FOUR GOSPELS

1. Relation to the rest of the Bible
   a. Old Testament promises a coming Redeemer; Gospels show fulfillment of this promise. They record His birth, ministry, death and resurrection. Also predict His second coming.
   b. Acts contains history of the Church from its founding on Day of Pentecost to Paul's first imprisonment in Rome (some 30 years).
   c. The epistles contain the distinctive teachings for the Church.
   d. The Revelation pictures Christ's second coming, and completes the prophetic picture of God's future program.

2. Relationship to each other
   "The Holy Spirit is not a reporter, but an editor." The Gospels are not attempts to give simple factual biographies of Jesus Christ; if so they would be very poor ones, as they tell only a very little of what He did. They are rather to emphasize four different aspects of His per-

son and work. At the time these records were committed to writing there were four principal groups of people: Jews, Romans, Greeks, and the rest of the world.

a. Matthew is the Gospel especially written for the Jews (Mal. 3:1). It presents Christ as the King, the promised Messiah.

b. Mark is the Gospel especially written for the Romans. It presents Christ as the suffering Servant of Jehovah, the accomplisher of mighty works. Key word, *straightway* used 40 times.

c. Luke is the Gospel written especially for the Greeks. It presents Christ as the perfect Man.

d. John is the Gospel written for all the world. It presents Christ as the Son of God who gave Himself for men because "God so loved the world" (John 3:16, key verse).

"Matthew is concerned with the coming of the promised Saviour; Mark with the life of a powerful Saviour; Luke with the grace of a perfect Saviour; John with the possession of a personal Saviour" (Griffith-Thomas).

Purpose of Christ's coming as indicated in each Gospel: Matthew 5:17—"to fulfill"; Mark 10:45—"to minister"; Luke 19:10—"to save"; John 5:43; 10:10—"to give life."

MATTHEW
Introduction

I. AUTHOR

No statement as to authorship in the book itself (title in Authorized Version not part of original text), but from earliest times there has been universal testimony that it was written by Matthew, one of the twelve Apostles. He is also called Levi. (Some think Matthew—"gift of God"—was a new name given him by Christ, as He named Simon, Peter. Compare Matt. 9:9 with Mark 2:14 and Luke 5:27-32). Matthew was a tax collector, a hated man. He helped the Romans to collect tribute from the Jews. None wanted to help the Gentiles, whom they expected to be swept from the land when Messiah came. Shows God's grace that a hated outcaste became the writer of the first book of the New Testament.

II. RECIPIENTS

Written especially to the Jews. Evidently written to those familiar with the Old Testament.

III. DATE

Some scholars set the date as early as A.D. 37, other conservative scholars as late as A.D. 68. Probably was the first Gospel written.

IV. PURPOSE

1. To prove that Jesus of Nazareth was the promised Messiah and King of Israel. More than 60 Old Testament references in Matthew.

2. To show how and why Jesus was rejected by
   Israel, and just what God's program is to be following that rejection.

V. THEME

The first coming and rejection of the promised
Messiah and King of Israel.

VI. KEY VERSES: 1:1; 23:37-39
    KEY WORDS: *Fulfilled* (with *fulfill*) —17 times
    Kingdom of Heaven—32 times

This expression found in Matthew only. Literally it is "kingdom of the heavens." Not synonymous
with "the Church." What did this mean to the
Jews of our Lord's day? They were looking for the
glorious earthly kingdom of Israel when the Messiah
would rule: the rule of the heavens on the earth
(Isa. 9:6, 7). This kingdom is announced first of
all as *at hand*. When it is rejected, the King then
gives a preview of the present age, during which
the Kingdom of Heaven exists in "mystery form"
(Matt. 13). It will be *literally* established when
Christ returns. This Gospel tells more of His return to reign than any other of the four (chs. 24,
25 especially).

Outline of Matthew

I. PREPARATION OF THE KING (Chs. 1-4)
   1. The genealogy of the King (1:1-17)
   2. The birth of the King (1:18-25)
   3. Wise Men seek the King to worship Him (2:
      1-12)

   4. The journey of the infant King to Egypt (2:13-23)
   5. The forerunner of the King (3:1-12)
   6. The baptism of the King (3:13-17)
   7. The testing of the King (4:1-11)
   8. Opening ministry and call of the first apostles (4:12-25)

II. PRESENTATION OF THE KING (Chs. 5-10)
   1. Proclamation of the King (chs. 5-7)
   2. Credentials of the King (chs. 8-9)
   3. Heralds of the King (ch. 10)

III. REJECTION OF THE KING (Chs. 11-23)
   1. Opposition to the King (chs. 11-12)
   2. Parables of the King (ch. 13)
   3. Definite rejection of the King (14:1—16:12)
   4. Instructions of the King (16:13—20:34)
   5. Final presentation and rejection of the King (chs. 21-23)

IV. PROPHECIES OF THE KING (Chs. 24-25)

V. DEATH AND RESURRECTION OF THE KING (Chs. 26-28)

MARK

Introduction

I. AUTHOR

As in other Gospels, the writer is not mentioned by name in the book, but strong tradition in Early Church ascribes it to Mark. Mark (also called John Mark in Acts 12:12, 25; 15:37) was related to Barnabas (cousin—Col. 4:10, R.V.) , a prominent leader in the Early Church. Mark accompanied Paul and Barnabas on their first missionary journey, but later was the cause of disagreement between the two missionaries (Acts 15:36-39). It is good to find that Paul speaks well of Mark much later (II Tim. 4:11).

Mark was not one of the twelve Apostles, but according to leaders in the Early Church he was a close companion of Peter, and his Gospel represents Peter's account of the various events. To bear this out, we find that he may have been a convert of Peter (I Peter 5:13); that Peter came to Mark's mother's house after being released from prison (Acts 12:12); that Peter is mentioned by name 23 times in the book.

II. Recipients

Probably intended originally to appeal to Romans. It is the briefest of the four Gospels and emphasizes actions rather than teaching. It presents Christ as the perfect and faithful Servant of Jehovah (Phil. 2:7. See also Isa. 42:1; 49:5-6; 52:13), the accomplisher of mighty works. Written for non-Jews evidently, as Jewish words and customs are explained (5:41; 7:1-4; 7:34; 14:12; 15:34, 42). Has nothing about genealogy, birth or infancy of our Lord. Has but a few Old Testament references (1:2-3; 15:28).

III. Date

Most modern scholars set date of writing between

A.D. 62-68. Some, however, place it as early as A.D. 40. It covers period of time from opening of John's ministry to ascension and early preaching of Apostles (about A.D. 25-32).

IV. PURPOSE

To present the Lord Jesus as the perfect and absolutely faithful Servant of Jehovah, so as to appeal especially to Roman people.

V. THEME

Jesus Christ, the Son of God, as the Suffering Servant of Jehovah (1:1; 9:37; 10:45)

VI. KEY VERSE: 10:45

KEY WORD: *Straightway*—40 times

(Note: In Authorized Version, *straightway*—19 times; *immediately*—15; *forthwith*—3; *as soon as*—2; *anon*—1; but all these translations represent the same Greek word.)

Multitude—17 times

Outline of Mark

I. THE PREPARATION OF THE SERVANT (1:1-13)
  1. The forerunner (vv. 1-8)
  2. The baptism, and witness of the Father (vv. 9-11)
  3. The temptation (vv. 12-13)

II. THE WORK OF THE SERVANT (1:14—8:26)
  1. Calls first disciples (1:14-20)
  2. Performs many miracles (1:21—3:12)
    Note frequent emphasis on presence of demons; their powerlessness before the Lord.

3. Apostles ordained, and scribes warned (3:13-35)
4. Four parables of the Lord (4:1-34)
   Compare—
   Matthew .... 21 miracles .... 15 parables
   Mark .... 19 miracles .... 5 parables
   Luke .... 20 miracles .... 19 parables
5. More mighty miracles (4:35—6:6)
6. The Apostles sent forth (6:7-31)
7. More mighty miracles (6:32—8:26)

III. THE SUFFERING OF THE SERVANT (8:27—15:47)
1. Suffering predicted (8:27—10:52)
2. Suffering caused by various things (11:1—13:37; "Suffer many things" 8:31). For example, barren fig tree (11:12-14); Temple conditions (11:15ff); opposition of leaders (11:27ff); by knowledge of Israel's future woes (13:1ff).
3. The suffering of death itself (14:1—15:47)
   a. Plotted (14:1-2)
   b. Anticipated (14:3-42)
   c. Consummated (14:43—15:47)

IV. THE VICTORY OF THE SERVANT (Ch. 16)
1. He rises from the dead (16:1-18)
2. He ascends to Heaven (16:19-20)

LUKE
Introduction

I. AUTHOR

Not mentioned by name in the book, but he does use first person in introduction (1:3). From earliest times universally considered to have been Luke (Col. 4:14). Some think that because of his name, his profession, the type of Greek used, and the person addressed, that Luke was a Greek himself, a Gentile Christian. Also separated from Jews in Colossians 4:10-14. He was not one of the twelve Apostles, but was a close associate of Paul (see "we" passages in Acts 16:9-12; 20:5—21:18; 27:1—28:16). Paul also mentions him in Philemon 24 and II Timothy 4:11.

II. RECIPIENTS

Addressed to Theophilus ("lover of God" or "loved by God") (1:3). Evidently he was a high official because called "most excellent" (cf. Acts 23:26; 24:3; 26:25). Though nothing further is known of him, evidently he was a Greek nobleman. Beyond this individual, the book seems to have been written especially for the Greeks, cultured people who loved beauty.

III. DATE

About A.D. 60 since it was written before Acts, which was written before Paul's death (about A.D. 68). Covers about 35 years, from the annunciation to Zacharias of John's birth to the ascension of Christ.

IV. PURPOSE

1. To present an accurate account of the facts about the life of Christ (1:1-4).
2. To present Christ as the perfect God-man, who

after a perfect ministry provided a perfect salvation for sinful humanity (19:10).

V. THEME

Christ the perfect Man as the Saviour of imperfect men.

VI. KEY VERSE: 19:10

KEY WORD: *Son of Man*—26 times. Speaks of more than just His humanity in contrast to His deity, "Son of God." It means He is the perfect, ideal Man, the true representative of the whole human race.

Outline of Luke

I. THE ANNOUNCEMENT AND ADVENT OF THE SON OF MAN (1:1—4:13)

1. Preface (1:1-4)
2. Announcement of the miraculous birth of the forerunner (1:5-25)
3. Annunciation of the birth of Jesus to Mary (1:26-38)
4. Mary visits her cousin Elisabeth (1:39-56)
5. Birth of John the Baptist (1:57-80)
6. Birth of Jesus, the Son of Man (2:1-20)
7. Circumcision of Jesus (2:21)
   Further shows His humanity.
8. Presentation of the infant Jesus at the temple (2:22-39)
9. Boyhood of Jesus (2:40-52)
   Shows again His complete humanity, yet even at 12 He appears as more than man.

10. The ministry of John the Baptist (3:1-20)

11. The baptism of the Son of Man (3:21-22)

12. The genealogy of the Son of Man (3:23-38)
    That of Mary. Joseph was thus "son-in-law"
    of Heli. Joseph's name used rather than Mary's
    in accordance with Jewish custom. Traces Je-
    sus back to Adam, as Son of Man.

13. Temptation of the Son of Man (4:1-13)
    As the perfect Man He must triumph where
    the first man Adam failed.

II. THE WORDS AND WORKS OF THE SON OF MAN
    (4:14—19:27)

  1. Rejected at Nazareth (4:14-30)
     They overemphasize His humanity, viewing
     Him as only an ordinary man.

  2. Teaches and heals in Galilee (4:31-44)

  3. Calls first disciples, heals leper and paralytic,
     and answers criticisms of scribes and Pharisees
     (ch. 5)

  4. The twelve disciples chosen and given teaching
     as to their conduct in the world (ch. 6)
     Is this part of "the Sermon on the Mount"?
     The Lord, like other great teachers, no doubt
     gave similar teaching on various occasions.
     Phrases are different here and no reference is
     made to the law (see v. 17).

  5. Performs wonderful miracles, relieves the doubts
     of John the Baptist, and visits in the home of a
     Pharisee (ch. 7).

6. Gives parables, stills the stormy sea, heals the sick and raises the dead (ch. 8).

7. Feeds the 5,000, is transfigured, announces His death (ch. 9).

8. Sends out the 70, denounces unbelieving cities, gives parable of the good Samaritan, visits Martha and Mary (ch. 10).

9. Various parables and other teachings (chs. 11-14)

10. The Lost Sheep, Lost Coin, Prodigal Son (ch. 15)
   All emphasize the joy over one lost but now found.

11. Instruction on various subjects (16:1—19:27)
   Also includes several miracles.

III. THE SUFFERING AND ATONING DEATH OF THE SON OF MAN (19:28—23:56)

1. The triumphal entry into Jerusalem and the cleansing of the Temple (19:28-48)

2. He answers well various tricky questions (ch. 20)

3. His last prophetic discourse (ch. 21)
   Luke, unlike Matthew, gives considerable material as to Christ's answers to the first question of verse 7.

4. The Last Supper, betrayal in the Garden of Gethsemane, the examination before the council (ch. 22)

5. The crucifixion and burial (ch. 23)

IV. THE RESURRECTION AND ASCENSION OF THE SON
    OF MAN (ch. 24)

JOHN

Introduction

I. AUTHOR

Believed to be John the apostle, son of Zebedee,
by the Early Church. John was one of the three
disciples closest to the Lord (Matt. 10:2; 17:1; Gal.
2:9). Note evidence for John's authorship in the
book itself. The book was evidently written by a
Jew (1:38; 4:9; 7:37, etc.). He was an eyewitness
of the events (1:14; 1:29; 1:35-36, etc.). John the
apostle is never called by name in the book when
referred to (1:40; 13:23; 21:20, 24) whereas all the
other three writers call him by name. Author speaks
of John the Baptist simply as John; other distinguished men who knew him vouched for it that the
writer was a disciple (21:24).

Additional facts about John: Family in good circumstances, as father had servants (Mark 1:20). He
and his brother were partners with Peter (Luke
5:10). He and his brother called "sons of thunder"
by the Lord (Mark 3:17); had a rather legalistic
spirit in the beginning (Luke 9:49, 51-56) and was
ambitious (Mark 10:35; cf. Matt. 20:20-21). Out-
ran Peter to tomb and is thought to have been
youngest disciple (20:4). Education limited (Acts
4:13). In later life, according to tradition, was the

leader of church at Ephesus, from which he was banished by Domitian to Patmos. Thought to have returned to Ephesus and died a natural death there. Also wrote three epistles and Revelation.

II. RECIPIENTS

No particular readers specified, but book has the whole world in view (1:9-12; 3:16; 17:18, 21, 23). Word *world* used 78 times

III. DATE

Second century is consistent that John wrote last to supply things lacking in the other three Gospels. Date was probably around A.D. 80-90. Book covers period from ministry of John the Baptist to the post-resurrection appearances of Christ, about five years.

IV. PURPOSE

To present Jesus as the Saviour of the world, the Son of God, so that men might believe on Him and be saved (20:31). To accomplish his purpose John does not attempt to tell all Jesus did and said, but selects certain items (20:30; 21:25).

V. THEME

Christ the Son of God who gave Himself for men, so that all who believe on Him may have eternal life.

VI. KEY VERSE: 3:16
KEY WORDS:
Father (God)	121 times
Love	57 times

World	78 times
Son (Christ)	42 times
Believe	98 times
Life	52 times

Outline of John

Note especially in John the seven signs (John 20: 30-31) of works before the resurrection:

1. Water to wine (2:1-11)
2. Nobleman's son healed (4:46-51)
3. Impotent man healed (5:1-9)
4. Feeding of 5,000 (6:1-14)
5. Walking on water (6:16-21)
6. Healing of blind man (9:1-7)
7. Resurrection of Lazarus (11:1-46)

Also the seven signs of words—"I am" (see Exodus 3:14):

1. Bread of life (6:35)
2. Light of the world (8:12)
3. Door (10:9)
4. Good shepherd (10:11)
5. Resurrection and life (11:25)
6. Way, truth and life (14:6)
7. Vine (15:1)

I. INTRODUCTION (Ch. 1)

II. PUBLIC MINISTRY OF THE SON OF GOD (Chs. 2-12)

Ch. 2 Water turned to wine at Cana; temple cleansed at Jerusalem

Ch. 3 Jesus and Nicodemus; further testimony from John the Baptist

Ch. 4 Jesus and the woman of Samaria; healing of the nobleman's son

Ch. 5 The impotent man healed and the critical Jews answered

Ch. 6 Jesus feeds the 5,000, walks on the sea, and reveals Himself as the Bread of Life

Ch. 7 The message of Jesus concerning the Holy Spirit, given at the Feast of Tabernacles

Ch. 8 The adulterous woman forgiven; the discourse on "the Light of the world'

Ch. 9 Healing of the blind man (an illustration of ch. 8)

Ch. 10 Discourse concerning the Good Shepherd

Ch. 11 Raising of Lazarus from the dead

Ch. 12 Supper at Bethany; public acclamation at Jerusalem; message concerning the "corn of wheat"

III. PRIVATE MINISTRY OF THE SON OF GOD (Chs. 13-17)

The teaching of our Lord to the disciples on the last night (chs. 14-16—"the upper room discourse" only in John)

Ch. 13 Jesus washes the disciples' feet; predicts His betrayal by Judas and denial by Peter

Ch. 14 The Lord speaks of His coming again, of His oneness with the Father, and promises to send the Holy Spirit

Ch. 15 The believer's relationship to Christ and to the world

Ch. 16 The work of the Holy Spirit with the world and with the believer

Ch. 17 The prayer of Christ for His own—really "the Lord's prayer"

IV. DEATH AND RESURRECTION OF THE SON OF GOD (Chs. 18-20)

Ch. 18 Jesus arrested in the garden of Gethsemane; taken before the high priest and Pilate

Ch. 19 Jesus condemned, crucified, and buried

Ch. 20 Jesus rises from the dead and appears to the disciples

V. CONCLUSION (Ch. 21)

Peter taught a lesson in Christian service by the risen Lord.

ACTS

Introduction

I. AUTHOR

Luke, the writer of the third Gospel. Even as in the Gospel, his name is not mentioned in Acts, but that both were written by the same author is shown by comparing Luke 1:1-4 with Acts 1:1-2. Medical terms used are also an additional proof of Luke's authorship (3:7; 9:18; 12:23; 13:11; 28:8, for example). He traveled with Paul on a number of occasions (II Tim. 4:11); note the "we" sections of Acts (16:9-12; 20:5—21:18; 27:1—28:16).

II. RECIPIENTS

Written originally to Theophilus, a high Gentile official who was also a Christian. Beyond this individual, it was written for the instruction of all who are interested in the beginning of the Church and the first outreach of the Gospel after the death, resurrection, and ascension of Christ.

III. DATE

About A.D. 63 (before Paul's death which was about A.D. 68). Covers a period of about 33 years, from the ascension of Christ to the time when Paul had been a prisoner in Rome for two years (A.D. 30-63).

IV. PURPOSE

To continue the record of the work of the Lord—this book contains the acts of the risen Lord (1:1).

It does not give the history of the work of each of the apostles as the title might indicate, but rather gives the beginning of the Church in certain places. Christ is still the center. This book shows that even though He has returned to Heaven yet He continues to work; directly, through the Holy Spirit who now has come in accordance with His promise, and through His own human servants whom He has sent out (John 17:18). Peter is the central human figure in the first 12 chapters; Paul in the last 16.

V. THEME

The beginning of the Church and the first outreach of the gospel "unto the uttermost part of the earth" as the believers witness in the power of the Holy Spirit.

VI. KEY VERSE: 1:8

KEY WORDS: *Name* (*name of Jesus, name of the Lord Jesus, My name,* etc.)   (examples 8:12; 9:15) —33 times

Spirit (referring to third Person of Trinity) with *Holy Ghost*—54 times

Outline of Acts

I. THE MINISTRY OF PETER AND OTHER BELIEVERS TO THE JEWS (Chs. 1-12)

Ch. 1 The ascension of Christ, and the choice of a successor to Judas

Ch. 2 The coming of the Holy Spirit and the beginning of the Church

Ch. 3 The lame man healed at the temple gate by Peter and John; Peter preaches to the curious crowd

Ch. 4 Peter and John arrested and threatened by the rulers; the disciples pray for boldness in witnessing

Ch. 5 Ananias and Sapphira smitten for lying to the Holy Spirit; the apostles are imprisoned, threatened, and beaten, but continue to witness for Christ

Ch. 6 Seven deacons selected to assist the apostles by caring for the daily ministration to the poor; one of these, Stephen, is mightily used of the Lord

Ch. 7 Stephen gives a message of condemnation to the council, and is stoned; first reference to Paul

Ch. 8 General persecution causes the believers to be scattered abroad; Samaria is evangelized by Philip and others

Ch. 9 The Lord speaks to Saul on the Damascus road; he is converted and preaches Christ; Peter heals Aeneas and raises the dead Dorcas

Ch. 10 Peter is divinely guided to preach the Gospel to the first Gentiles; Cornelius and family are saved

Ch. 11 Peter answers criticism of his preaching to

Cornelius; Barnabas and Saul minister to the church at Antioch

Ch. 12 Herod kills James and imprisons Peter; Peter delivered by an angel; Herod dies a terrible death

II. THE MINISTRY OF PAUL TO THE GENTILES (Chs. 13-28)

Ch. 13 Paul and Barnabas are sent by the Holy Spirit on their first missionary journey; they sail to Cyprus, then back to the mainland, where they receive a wide hearing in Antioch, but are opposed by the jealous Jews

Ch. 14 They preach at Iconium; Paul heals the crippled man at Lystra, but is later stoned there; the apostles finally return to Antioch after a profitable trip

Ch. 15 The council at Jerusalem repudiates the Judaizers; Paul and Silas set out on a second missionary journey

Ch. 16 Paul directed to Macedonia in Europe; his ministry at Philippi

Ch. 17 Paul preaches at Thessalonica, Berea and Athens

Ch. 18 Paul at Corinth and Ephesus, then returns to Antioch; sets out on a third missionary journey

(Note his method of working in the great

centers; then converts carried the Gospel to outlying districts.)

Ch. 19 He ministers in Ephesus for three years (20:31) ; Demetrius raises a riot there against him

Ch. 20 Paul again works in Macedonia and Greece, then returns to Troas and Miletus; gives a farewell message to the Ephesian elders

Ch. 21 Paul goes to Jerusalem; is seized by a mob while worshiping in the temple

Ch. 22 Paul speaks to the mob

Ch. 23 Paul before the council; sent to Caesarea to Felix the Roman governor

Ch. 24 Paul testifies before Felix

Ch. 25 Paul is brought before Festus and Agrippa

Ch. 26 Paul testifies before Festus and Agrippa

Ch. 27 Paul is sent by sea to Rome, and suffers shipwreck

Ch. 28 Paul winters at Melita (Malta), then travels on to Rome where the Jews hear his message; he stays in Rome two years enjoying considerable liberty

The Pauline Epistles

Introduction

I. AUTHOR

The apostle Paul, formerly Saul of Tarsus. One can better understand the teachings of the great Apostle to the Gentiles when the three divisions of his career are kept in mind:

1. His early life. By birth a Jew, by training a Hebrew of the Hebrews, largely influenced by the Pharisees, yet thoroughly acquainted with Greek culture and possessing Roman citizenship. A brilliant, highly educated man who was a "conscientious objector" to Christianity.

2. His wonderful conversion, when he saw the resurrected Christ on the road to Damascus.

3. His close walk with Christ and fruitful ministry during the last 30 years of his life.

Thirteen New Testament epistles were written by him and bear his name in first verse. One epistle (Hebrews) bears no name, but is thought by many to be Pauline in authorship.

II. RECIPIENTS

Eight epistles were written originally to individual local churches: two each to the churches at Corinth and Thessalonica; one each to the churches at Rome, Ephesus, Philippi, Colosse.

One was written to a group of churches: Galatians.

Four to individuals: two to Timothy; one each to Titus and Philemon.

Hebrews to an unnamed group of Jewish Christians.

III. DATES

Saul converted—A.D. 35

First missionary journey—A.D. 45-50

Second missionary journey—A.D. 51-54

I Thessalonians thought to be earliest epistle— about A.D. 52

Third missionary journey—A.D. 54-58

II Timothy thought to be the last epistle—about A.D. 67

IV. PURPOSE

To present the needed truths concerning the Church as the body of Christ: "its membership, privileges, responsibilities, and destiny" (Springer).

V. THEME:

The Church

VI. KEY VERSES: Ephesians 3:1-12

I Corinthians 12:12-27

KEY WORDS:

Church—64 times (including Hebrews)

Grace—97 times (including Hebrews)

Gospel—68 times (including Hebrews)

Faith—167 times (including Hebrews)

ROMANS
Introduction

I. **AUTHOR**

Paul the apostle (1:1).

II. **RECIPIENTS**

The church at Rome (1:6-7, 15). No one knows when this church was founded or by whom. Paul had not been there personally, but had long desired to visit the world metropolis (1:9-13; 15:22-29); indeed felt such a visit to be the divine intention (Acts 19:21), though he little realized that he would make this visit as a prisoner.

III. **DATE**

A number of factors indicate Corinth as the place of writing (16:1, 2). Probably written during Paul's second visit to Corinth (about A.D. 58).

IV. **PURPOSE**

1. Paul writes this epistle to reveal his desire to visit Rome and to pave the way for his eventual coming (1:10; 15:24).

2. Paul also desires to have an immediate written ministry, since his personal ministry has been providentially hindered (1:13).

3. The Roman church was apparently predominantly Gentile (cf. names in ch. 16), but there were evidently also Jewish believers (see 7:1; 11:13) and the question of the rejection of Christianity by the Jews and God's future purpose for Israel was of pressing importance. The

answer to this question is given at length in chapters 9-11.

4. At the same time legalistic Judaizers were probably attempting to deceive the people (as they had recently done in Galatia and earlier in Antioch), and a clear exposition of justification by faith was needed by this church, which was located in such a strategic position (Rom. 16:17-19).

V. THEME

The Gospel of Christ

VI. KEY VERSES: 1:16-17

KEY WORDS: *Justify* (and *justification*) —17 times

Faith—37 times

Christ—39 times

Outline of Romans

I. INTRODUCTION (1:1-17)

II. DOCTRINAL (1:18—8:39)

  1. Necessity of the Gospel (1:18—3:20)

    a. Condition of the immoral, idolatrous heathen world (1:18-32)

    b. Condition of the cultured and moral Gentile (2:1-16)

    c. Condition of the self-righteous Jew (2:17-29)

    d. The condition of all humanity (3:1-20)

  2. Justification by faith (3:21—5:21)

    a. Righteousness obtained through faith in Jesus Christ (3:21-31)

    b. The witness of the Old Testament (4:1-25)

   c. The results of justification by faith (5:1-11)
   d. The two heads and the results of their two
      acts (5:12-21)
3. Victory over sin in the believer's life (6:1—
   8:39)
   a. The believer to have victory over sin be-
      cause of union with Christ in death and
      resurrection (6:1-23)
   b. The believer not under law (7:1-6)
   c. The victorious Christian life does not come
      through the law (7:7-25)
   d. Victory through the law of the Spirit of life
      (8:1-13)
   e. The result of "life after the Spirit" (8:14-
      39)

III. DISPENSATIONAL (Chs. 9-11)
   1. Israel's past—God's mercy shown to Israel has
      always been on the basis of His sovereignty
      (ch. 9)
   2. Israel's present—God's discipline at work (ch.
      10)
   3. Israel's future—national restoration (ch. 11)

IV. PRACTICAL (12:1—15:13)
   1. The Christian life in relation to self (12:1-2)
   2. The Christian life in relation to the Body of
      Christ (12:3-16)
   3. The Christian life in relation to all mankind
      (12:17-21)

4. The Christian life in relation to earthly government (13:1-14)
5. The Christian life in relation to doubtful matters and weaker brethren (14:1—15:3)
6. Joy, peace and hope for all—both Jew and Gentile—in Christ (15:4-13)

V. CONCLUSION (15:14—16:27)
1. Paul's desire for spiritual blessing for the recipients (15:14-33)
2. Personal greetings and parting exhortations (16:1-27)

I CORINTHIANS
Introduction

I. AUTHOR
Paul the apostle (1:1).

II. RECIPIENTS
The church at Corinth (1:2). Paul also intended that this letter circulate beyond this particular church, to "all that in every place call upon the name of Jesus our Lord." In Paul's day, Corinth was an important commercial center, having a population of 600,000 or 700,000. It was a Grecian city, noted as a sport center (I Cor. 9:24-27). Morals were low; there was a temple to Aphrodite, the goddess of beauty, in connection with which there were about 1000 women prostitutes. It was a great temptation to the Corinthian Christians to be lax in their morals. Paul's work at Corinth during his second

missionary journey is recorded in Acts 18:1-18. He spent more than a year and a half there (Acts 18:11, 18). Many turned to the Lord (Acts 18:9-10).

III. DATE

Written from Ephesus (16:7-8) about A.D. 57, during Paul's third missionary journey. Later he visited Corinth again (Acts 20:1-2).

IV. PURPOSE

1. To answer questions the Corinthians had addressed to him concerning problems in the church (7:1; cf. also 8:1; 12:1; 16:1). These problems in one form or another are more or less common to all churches.

2. To reprove a spirit of contentious factionalism in the church, the result of following various human teachers (I Cor. 1:11-13).

3. To defend his apostleship and ministry, which were being attacked by the Judaizers (I Cor. 9).

V. THEME

Errors of Christian conduct corrected

VI. KEY VERSES: 14:33, 40

Outline of I Corinthians

INTRODUCTION (1:1-9)

1. Salutation (1:1-3)
2. Thanksgiving (1:4-9)

I. ERRORS CORRECTED: DIVISIONS (1:10—4:16)

1. Existence of divisions (1:10-17)

2. Man's Wisdom Versus God's Wisdom (1:18-25) (Their divisions came from following human wisdom.)

3. God sets aside man's wisdom (1:26-31)

4. The central theme of God's wisdom and of Paul's preaching (2:1-5)

5. God's wisdom revealed to us by the Holy Spirit (2:6-13)

6. Men's condition is made clear by their reception of God's wisdom (2:14-16)

7. The Corinthians are carnal—saved but following man's wisdom, not God's (3:1-9)

8. Building on the true foundation (3:10-15)

9. Warning against the destruction of God's temple (3:16-17)

10. The Christian's limitations and resources (3:18-23)

11. God's stewards (4:1-5)

12. The apostolic example (4:6-16)

II. ERRORS CORRECTED: IMMORALITY (4:17—6:20)

1. Godly life the test of profession (4:17-21)

2. "Purge out the old leaven" (5:1-8)

3. Christian fellowship limited (5:9-13)

4. Christians warned against going to law (6:1-11)

5. The highest appeal for purity (6:12-20)

III. ERRORS CORRECTED: CONCERNING MARRIAGE (Ch. 7)

1. Responsibilities of marriage (7:1-7)

   2. Instructions to the married (7:8-24)

   3. Advice to the single and to the married (7:25-40)

IV. ERRORS CORRECTED: CONCERNING CHRISTIAN LIBERTY (chs. 8-11)

   1. Regarding idols and meat offered to them (our attitude toward things harmless in themselves but with an evil connotation to others) (8:1-13)

   2. Liberty in the ministry (9:1-23)

   3. Running the race—self-discipline of the Christians (9:24-27)

   4. Examples from Israel's history (10:1-13)

   5. Christian liberty and the Lord's Table (10:14-33)

   6. Instructions regarding modesty in women (11:1-6)

   7. Instructions regarding the Lord's Supper (11:17-34)

V. ERRORS CORRECTED: CONCERNING SPIRITUAL GIFTS (Chs. 12-14)

   1. Spiritual gifts sovereignly controlled by the Holy Spirit (12:1-11)

   2. The Body of Christ compared to the human body (12:12-31)

   3. The more excellent way—that of love (ch. 13)

   4. The greatest gift—that of prophecy (14:1-40)

VI. ERRORS CORRECTED: CONCERNING THE GOSPEL (Ch. 15)

VII. ERRORS CORRECTED: CONCERNING MONEY (16: 1-9)

CLOSING ADMONITIONS (16:10-24)

II CORINTHIANS
Introduction

I. AUTHOR
Paul the apostle (1:1)

II. RECIPIENTS
The church at Corinth (1:1; 6:11). Same church to which the previous epistle was directed. Also intended this letter to circulate throughout all Greece (Achaia): "with all the saints which are in all Achaia."

III. DATE
Written not long after I Corinthians. Probably in the latter part of A.D. 57, after Paul had left Ephesus and while he was somewhere in Macedonia. Paul had sent Titus to Corinth while still in Ephesus.

IV. PURPOSE
Paul had been in great danger in Ephesus, from which city he had written I Corinthians (II Cor. 1:8). He had gone on to Troas (II Cor. 2:12), where he had expected to meet Titus, but did not find him there (II Cor. 2:13). From there he went on to Macedonia, where Titus met him and brought him a generally favorable report as to the conduct

of the Corinthians after receiving his previous letter
(7:5-11) . However, some things still needed to be
said.

1. He is afraid lest they be too severe with the
   chief offender mentioned in I Corinthians (II
   Cor. 2:5-11) .
2. He wants to give further instruction about the
   offering they are raising for the poor saints at
   Jerusalem (9:1-5) .
3. He wishes to defend his apostleship and authority against false teachers who seek to establish
   themselves by criticizing him (10:10; 11:4, 13-
   15; 12:12; 13:3) .

V. THEME
  The true gospel ministry for Christ

VI. KEY VERSES: 4:5; 5:20-21
     KEY WORDS: Different forms of the word *minis-
     try*—18 times
     Glory, boast (same Greek word)—20 times
  (Comparison is made between that in which the
false teacher glories and that in which the true minister of Christ glories—10:17.)

Outline of II Corinthians

I. THE MINISTRY OF RECONCILIATION (see 5:18)—
    PRINCIPLES OF A TRUE GOSPEL MINISTRY (Chs.
    1-7)
    1. Introduction (1:1-11)
    2. His conscience is clear; he postponed his in-

tended visit to Corinth not because of light-
ness, but to spare them embarrassment (1:12—
2:4)

3. He appeals for a reinstatement of the repentant
offender (II Cor. 2:5-13; cf. I Cor. 5:1)

4. The first characteristic of true Gospel ministry:
continual triumph, as we make manifest the
sweetness of God's knowledge (2:14-17)

5. A true Gospel ministry proves itself by changed
lives (3:1-5)

6. The true Gospel ministry far more glorious
than that of the old covenant (3:6-18)

7. The message of the true Gospel ministry (4:
1-6)

8. The power of the true Gospel ministry (4:7-15)

9. The hope of the true Gospel ministry (4:16—
5:10)

10. The motives of the true Gospel ministry (5:
11-16)   (Fear of God and love of Christ)

11. The nature of the true Gospel ministry (5:
17-21)

12. The trials of the true Gospel ministry (6:1-10)

13. The call to separation (6:11—7:1)

14. The joy of the apostle over the Corinthians'
conduct (7:2-16)

II. THE MINISTRY OF GIVING: TRUE CHRISTIAN
LIBERALITY (Chs. 8-9)

1. The good example of the Macedonians (8:1-6)

2. The supreme example of Christ (8:7-9)

3. Advice concerning giving (8:10—9:5)
4. The happy results of liberality (9:6-15)

III. THE MINISTRY OF THE APOSTLE—VINDICATION
OF PAUL'S AUTHORITY (Chs. 10-13)
1. Paul asserts his apostolic authority (ch. 10)
2. Paul's reason for asserting his authority (11:1-15)
(False apostles seek to undermine confidence in
Paul so as to lead the people astray from the simple
Gospel message.)
3. Paul's sufferings for Christ are a further proof
of his apostleship (11:16-33). His life itself
gives testimony to his sincerity.
4. Paul's visions and revelations are a still further
proof of his apostleship (12:1-10)
5. Paul's unselfish love for the Corinthians a
further proof of his apostleship (12:11-18)
6. Paul will manifest his apostolic authority when
he comes again (12:19—13:10)
7. Conclusion (13:11-14)

GALATIANS

Introduction

I. AUTHOR
Paul the apostle (1:1; 5:2).

II. RECIPIENTS
The churches of Galatia (1:2; 3:1). Galatia was
a Roman province in central Asia Minor. Paul

visited this section at least twice—with Silas on the
second missionary journey (Acts 16:6), and again
at the beginning of his third journey (Acts 18:23).
The Galatian people were Gauls, who had originally migrated there from western Europe. As a people, they were warm-hearted and generous (4:15),
but fickle and easily misled (1:6; 3:1, 3); also in-
clined to be quarrelsome (5:15).

III. DATE

Probably written from Ephesus (Acts 18:23; 19:1)
about A.D. 55-56.

IV. PURPOSE

The Judaizers mentioned in Acts 15:1 had continued to work. They had tried to obstruct the
work of Paul in various places and had been particu-
larly successful in Galatia (1:6-7; 4:17; 5:12; 6:12-
13). Their error was not so much substituting works
for faith, but rather attempting to combine works
and faith. (They said that a sinner was saved by
faith plus works, and that the saved were to be perfected through works as they kept the Mosaic Law.)
Paul writes:

1. To defend the true Gospel.
2. To expose and condemn this false teaching.
3. To show the true purpose of the law.
4. To show how the believer is to be perfected in
   the Christian life by walking in the Spirit
   (5:16).

V. THEME
Christian liberty defended

VI. KEY VERSE: 5:1
KEY WORDS: *Law*—32 times
Faith—21 times

Outline of Galatians

I. PAUL DEFENDS HIS MESSAGE AND APOSTLESHIP
(Chs. 1-2)

1. Salutation (1:1-5)
Very brief. Contains no thanksgiving, as most
of the other letters. Paul rushes right into his
main subject with great intensity of feeling.
(Even in verse 1 he speaks of his authority.)
Harder on them for doctrinal error than on
Corinthians for errors of conduct.

2. Condemnation of those who pervert the Gospel (1:6-9)

3. Paul's Gospel message not a human production,
but given to him by divine revelation (1:10-
14)

4. Paul's apostleship came directly from God, not
from the other apostles at Jerusalem (1:15-24)

5. Paul's apostleship confirmed by the other apostles at Jerusalem (2:1-10)

6. Paul's rebuke of Peter at Antioch shows his in-
dependent authority (2:11-21)

II. PAUL SHOWS THE CONTRAST BETWEEN LAW AND
GRACE (Chs. 3-4)

1. Results of the law and of faith (3:1-14)
    a. The Holy Spirit given not by the law but
       through faith (vv. 1-5)
    b. Righteousness (justification) comes through
       faith, not the law (vv. 6-9)
    c. The law curses—Christ redeems us from the
       curse (vv. 10-14) Why seek to put our-
       selves back under the law again and under
       the curse after being redeemed through
       faith?

2. The law cannot disannul the promise made to
   Abraham (3:15-18) This promise, which lays
   the basis for the Gospel, came long before the
   law was given, so the law cannot cancel or
   add anything to it.

3. The real purpose of the law (3:19-25)
   It was added not to provide a way of salvation,
   but (v. 19) to show man his transgressions, his
   true moral condition. It was given to the Jews
   as a schoolmaster (child trainer) to lead them
   to Christ (v. 24). Now that faith has come—
   that Christ has been fully revealed and the
   Gospel clearly made known—there is no further
   need for the schoolmaster⁻ (v. 25).

4. Faith in Christ brings us to the position of sons
   of God (3:26-29). The law can add nothing
   to this.

5. The wonderful position of believers as sons of

God (4:1-7)

6. In turning from the Gospel to the law, they are turning back to forms and ceremonies for salvation even as during their heathen days (4:8-20)

7. An allegory (4:21-31). The sons of the bondwoman (law) may appear to be sons of Abraham, but the true sons of Abraham are the sons of promise (faith). The two cannot get along together; the bondwoman and her son must be cast out.

III. PAUL SHOWS THE TRUE METHOD OF HOLY LIVING FOR THE BELIEVER (Chs. 5-6)

1. The Galatians are exhorted to stand fast in their Christian liberty (5:1-12)

2. Christian liberty, however, is not to be used as an excuse for wickedness (5:13-15)

3. The true method of holy living is to walk in the Spirit (5:16-26)

4. The way in which a sinful brother is to be treated under grace (6:1-5)

5. The principle of sowing and reaping is still true under grace (6:6-10)

6. Conclusion (6:11 18)

EPHESIANS

Introduction

I. AUTHOR

Paul the Apostle (1:1; 3:1)

II. RECIPIENTS

The church at Ephesus (1:1). Ephesus was the chief city of the Roman province of Asia (which comprised the western third of what we now call Asia Minor.) As a city, it was exceptionally blessed of God during the opening years of the present dispensation. Paul spent no less than three years laboring there (Acts 20:31). The record of this ministry is found in Acts 19. After his departure he sent Timothy to continue the work (I Tim. 1:3). Other notable Christian leaders also ministered in Ephesus—Aquila, Priscilla, Apollos. The present epistle, as well as Paul's parting message to the elders of Ephesus (Acts 20:17-38), makes it clear that the Word of God fell indeed on fertile soil at Ephesus, producing much fruit. Tradition indicates that the apostle John also made it the center of his labors during the latter years of his life (Rev. 2:1-7).

The apostle Paul, in writing this letter, also had in view all "the faithful in Christ Jesus" (1:1), that is, all believers everywhere (cf. Gal. 3:9).

III. DATE

Apparently written while Paul was a prisoner at Rome (3:1; 4:1; 6:20; Acts 28:16, 30-31), about A.D. 62.

IV. PURPOSE

1. Paul desires to strengthen these believers in their Christian faith (3:16-19)

2. He wishes to encourage them to turn away from the things of the old life and to "put on the new man" (4:17-24 and ff.)

3. He writes to show them the unity of both Jews and Gentiles in the body of Christ (2:14-18), and to reveal the glorious position of the believer as a member of the Body of Christ (1:3; 4:1).

V. THEME

The heavenly position of the believer as a member of the Body of Christ and the daily life which corresponds to this position.

VI. KEY VERSES: 1:3; 4:1

KEY WORDS: *In*—93 times (89 times in Greek) — very important—shows the real secret of the spiritual life. We are "in Christ" (1:1) —"in the heavenlies" (1:3).

Grace—12 times

Body—8 times (used of the Church—an organism)

Walk—8 times (the way we should live because of our position)

Outline of Ephesians

I. THE POSITION OF THE BELIEVER ("IN THE HEAVENLIES IN CHRIST") (Chs. 1-3)

1. Salutation (1:1-2)

2. The believer's spiritual blessings in Christ (1:3-14)

a. Statement regarding the blessings (v. 3)

b. The Father's part in our blessings (vv. 4-6)

c. The Son's part in our blessings (vv. 7-12)

d. The Holy Spirit's part in our blessings (vv. 13-14)

3. The first prayer of the apostle (1:15-23)
This prayer is that the believers may have wisdom to know what the Father has made the Lord Jesus Christ to be unto His people.

4. The past, present and future of the believer (2:1-10)

5. Both Jews and Gentiles are one in Christ and form a living temple of God (2:11-22)

6. The revelation of the mystery (3:1-12)

7. The second prayer of the apostle (3:13-21)
That believers may know what God has provided for them in Christ.

II. THE WALK OF THE BELIEVER (4:1—6:9)

1. The believer should endeavor to keep the unity of the Spirit (4:1-6)

2. The believer should use the gifts given him for the edifying (building up) of the Body of Christ (4:7-16)

3. The believer is not to walk as the Gentiles walk (4:17-32)

4. The believer is to walk as a dear child imitating his heavenly Father (5:1-14)

5. The believer to have a Spirit-filled walk (5:15-21)

6. Special instructions for wives, husbands, children, fathers, servants, and masters (5:22—6:9)

III. THE WARFARE OF THE BELIEVER (6:10-24)

PHILIPPIANS

Introduction

I. AUTHOR

Paul the apostle (1:1). Links Timothy with himself, but evidently the sole writer, as he speaks in the first person throughout.

II. RECIPIENTS

"All the saints in Christ Jesus at Philippi," or the church at Philippi. The church equals "all the saints." *Saint* means one set apart for holy fellowship and service. Refers to position not to experience. However, we should ever seek to live in accordance with our position. Especially addressed are the bishops (note plural) and deacons of this church. Bishop is "overseer," and evidently refers to same office at that of elder. *Deacon* means servant, but a voluntary one. Refers to those who handled temporal affairs of church.

Philippi was an ancient city of Macedonia. Formerly called by another name, but in 356 B.C. annexed by Philip of Macedon (father of Alexander the Great) and called by his name (Philippi, "pertaining to Philip"). Later became a Roman colony (Acts 16:12), which meant it was considered a portion of Rome itself transplanted to the colonies. Its inhabitants thus became Roman citizens, governed by their own senate and judges, and not under the control of the governor of the province. People were very proud of these rights, which explains why they were so easily moved against Paul and Silas by the accusation of Acts 16:20, 21. Paul doubtless had this in mind also in use of certain terms, such as Philippians 3:20.

The dramatic founding of this church is recorded in Acts 16. This took place on Paul's second missionary journey, about A.D. 51. Three particular converts are mentioned in Acts 16: a Jewess (or Jewish proselyte—Lydia), a Greek slave girl, a Roman official. The Gospel works with all classes and races. Paul speaks of his sufferings at Philippi in I Thessalonians 2:2. The people there loved him and sent supplies for his material needs; twice they did this while he was at Thessalonica (Phil. 4:15-16), and still a third time while he was at Corinth, just before he wrote this epistle to them (II Cor. 11:9; Phil. 4:10, 18).

III. DATE

About A.D. 63 or 64. Written from Rome (4:22; 1:13; cf. Acts 28:16). Written near the end of Paul's first imprisonment.

IV. PURPOSE

The Philippians had heard of Paul's imprisonment and had sent a gift to him by the hand of

Epaphroditus (4:18). While in Rome, Epaphroditus became seriously ill, and news of this went back to the Philippians. Word came back to Rome that they had received this news and were greatly concerned. This caused Epaphroditus to be grieved, and since he was now well Paul sent him on to the Philippians again to advise them that he himself hoped to follow (2:24-30). This means at least four trips over the 700 miles separating Rome and Philippi—a journey of at least a month. Since Paul lived in Rome two years (Acts 28:30), the time must have been nearly up.

There was no serious doctrinal error in Philippi evidently. The letter was written:

1. To thank the people for their gifts

2. To advise them of Paul's intended visit

3. To encourage them to go on with Christ

4. To warn them against false Judaizing teachers (ch. 3)

5. To advise concerning a difference of opinion between two of the women, Euodias and Syntyche (ch. 4).

V. THEME

Rejoicing in the Lord (1:26; 3:1, 3; 4:4, 10) or the joyful Christian experience.

VI. KEY VERSE: 4:4

KEY WORD: *Joy* (with *rejoicing*) —18 times

Outline of Philippians

I. REJOICING IN THE PROGRESS OF THE GOSPEL (Ch. 1)
   1. Salutation (vv. 1-2)
   2. Praise and prayer (vv. 3-11)
   3. Progress of the Gospel in spite of persecution and false motives (vv. 12-18)
   4. Paul's determination that Christ shall be magnified "by life or by death" (vv. 19-26)
   5. Paul's joy in the witness of faithful believers (vv. 27-30)

II. REJOICING IN SACRIFICIAL SERVICE (Ch. 2)
   1. Importance of humility (vv. 1-11)
   2. Joy found in "holding forth the Word of life" in sacrificial service (vv. 12-18)
   3. Further examples of sacrificial service: Timothy "an unselfish pastor" and Epaphroditus "a devoted messenger" (vv. 19-30)

III. REJOICING IN THE PROPER PERSON (Ch. 3)
   Not in self—the flesh—but in the Lord
   1. Paul, the Christian's example (vv. 1-17)
   2. Friends and enemies of Christ (vv. 18-21)

IV. REJOICING IN THE PEACE OF GOD (Ch. 4)
   1. The peace of unity among brethren (vv. 1-3)
   2. The peace of complete trust in God (vv. 4-7)
   3. The peace of purity of mind (vv. 8-9)
   4. The peace of contentment in any state (vv. 10-12)

5. The peace of dependence on the strength of Christ (vv. 13-20)
6. Conclusion (vv. 21-23)

COLOSSIANS
Introduction

I. AUTHOR

Paul the apostle (1:1, 23; 4:18). Links Timothy with himself in 1:1 but evidently the sole writer as he speaks often in the first person (1:25, 29; 4:7, 8, etc.).

II. RECIPIENTS

"The saints and faithful brethren in Christ which are at Colosse" (1:2) —the church at Colosse. A large city on the Lycus River in the district of Phrygia, is in what we call Asia Minor. It was 100 miles east of Ephesus and only 10 miles from Laodicea and 13 from Hierapolis (see 4:13, 16). There is no record in Acts of Paul's visiting Colosse, and he evidently did not found the church there (2:1). Perhaps Epaphras did (1:7; 4:12, 13). Philemon lived there (4:9 with Philem. 10, 23; also Philem. 2 with 4:17) and the church met at his house. Others, however, met at another home (4:15).

III. DATE

Written about the same date as Ephesians (A.D. 62) while Paul was in his first imprisonment at Rome (Col. 1:24; 4:18; Eph. 3:1; Col. 4:10; Philem. 9).

IV. Purpose

Although he had not visited Colosse, Paul learned of the church there from Epaphras (1:7), who was apparently imprisoned with him at Rome (Philem. 23). He sends this letter to them by Tychicus (4:7-9), who is accompanied by Onesimus (Philem. 10-12). Paul himself hopes to visit them later (Philem. 22). He writes to them in order to warn them against errors of doctrine and practice.

1. To warn them against human philosophy and to urge them to give Christ the supreme place (2:8-10; 1:18).
2. To warn them against ritualism (2:16). Judaizers evidently present here too.
3. To warn them against the worship of angels and false mysticism (2:18-19).
4. To warn them against asceticism (2:20-23). Asceticism: "Doctrine that through self-torture or self-denial, one can discipline himself to reach a high state, spiritually or intellectually" (Webster).

   In this church the people had a tendency to place too much emphasis on human wisdom and ordinances, and not to give Christ the supreme place He should have.

V. Theme

The pre-eminence of Christ (1:15-19). He is pictured not only as the Head of the Church, but of the whole universe.

VI. KEY VERSES: 1:18; 2:10.
   KEY WORD: *Head*—3 times

Outline of Colossians

I. THE SUPREME GLORY OF CHRIST (Ch. 1)
   1. Salutation (vv. 1, 2)
   2. Thanksgiving (vv. 3-8)
   3. The apostle's prayer (vv. 9-14)
   4. The supreme glory of the person of Christ (vv. 15-19)
   5. The supreme glory of the work of Christ (vv. 20-29)

II. WARNING AGAINST ERROR (Ch. 2)
   1. Warning against being beguiled with enticing words (vv. 1-7)
   2. Warning against mere human wisdom and worldly teachings (vv. 8-10)
   3. Warning against ritualism (vv. 11-17)
   4. Warning against worshiping angels and false mysticism (vv. 18, 19)
   5. Warning against asceticism (vv. 20-23)

III. THE NEW LIFE IN CHRIST (Ch. 3)
   1. True separation (vv. 1-4)
   2. Warning against vile sins (vv. 5-7)
   3. Warning against more respectable sins (vv. 8-9)
   4. Instruction as to the positive Christian virtues (vv. 10-17)
   5. Instruction for various classes of Christians (vv. 18-25)

IV. THE NEW FELLOWSHIP IN CHRIST (Ch. 4)
  1. Instruction for masters (v. 1)
  2. A general exhortation to all (vv. 2-6)
  3. Paul's fellow workers (vv. 7-18)

I THESSALONIANS

Introduction

I. AUTHOR

Paul the apostle (1:1; 2:18). Paul links Silas (Silvanus) and Timothy (Timotheus) with himself in the first verse, but this does not mean that the authorship was joint (see 2:18; 3:5; 5:27). He links their names with his because they had a part with him in founding the church at Thessalonica and shared his interest and concern in the work. When he says "we" (1:2) he doubtless speaks for all three.

II. RECIPIENTS

The church of the Thessalonians (1:1). Paul was beaten and imprisoned at Philippi, but a real work of the Lord was done there (Acts 16). He, Silas, and Timothy then left Philippi and went about 100 miles southwest in Macedonia to Thessalonica (Acts 17:1), a large and influential city of that day (still an important town in Greece; modern name, Salonika). The city had been located in a rich plains section, and had an excellent harbor, so grew quickly. Thessalonica differed considerably from Philippi; the latter was a Roman colony, while the former was predominantly Greek in culture. At the time

Paul visited there, the city had a population consisting of native Greeks, Roman colonists, Asiatic people, and a large number of Jews. Paul spent only about three weeks in the city (Acts 17:2), with the result that a large number were converted both of Jews and Gentiles (Acts 17:3-5). The unbelieving Jews then raised a riot against Paul, who deemed it best to depart for a time, and so went on to Berea, 50 miles southwest of Thessalonica (Acts 17:5-10).

III. DATE

Probably around A.D. 52. Paul earnestly desired to visit Thessalonica again (I Thess. 2:18; 3:10). This not being possible, he sent Timothy from Athens (I Thess. 3:1, 2), who brought back a good report to Paul (I Thess. 3:6). This came to him while he was at Corinth (Acts 18:1, 5), where he stayed for a year and a half. This report was the occasion for his writing this letter. It is thought to be the first of his epistles from point of time.

IV. PURPOSE

The state of this church in general was very good; however, there were certain things that needed correction:

1. Some were seeking to undermine the influence of the apostle, accusing him of false teaching, of immoral teaching, of hypocrisy (2:3; cf. Rom. 3:8).

2. These slanderers apparently indicated that

Paul was afraid to return. He writes to assure that such is not the case (2:17-18).

3. Paul was also accused of being greedy, seeking money, and using flattery (2:5, 6).

4. There was danger of cliques, as in Corinth (5:13, 20, 26, 27).

5. There was confusion over questions connected with the second coming of Christ (4:11-18; 5:1-6).

On the positive side Paul writes:

6. To encourage the Thessalonians in persecution (2:14).

7. To exhort them lest they slip back into heathen immorality (4:3-8).

V. THEME

The second coming of Christ (mentioned in each chapter) (1:10; 2:12, 19; 3:13: 4:13-18; 5:1-11, 23)

VI. KEY VERSES: 1:9, 10

KEY WORDS: *Coming* (of the Lord) —4 times
Comfort—6 times

Outline of I Thessalonians

Two main divisions, each closing with a benediction.

I. PERSONAL—PAUL'S PAST AND PRESENT DEALINGS WITH THE THESSALONIAN CHURCH (Ch. 1-3)

1. Greeting (1:1)

2. Thanksgiving (1:2-10)

When Paul commends his friends for their

good works, he does it in the form of a thanks-giving to God!

3. The ministry of the apostles (2:1-20)

An ideal ministry—"an admirable message for the guidance of ministers and missionaries and Christian workers in modern times" (Erdman). Applies "not only to public servants, but to every follower of Christ."

a. As evangelists (vv. 1-6)
b. As pastors (vv. 7-9)
c. As teachers (vv. 10-12)
d. The result of the apostles' ministry (vv. 13-16)
e. Satanic opposition to the ministry (vv. 17-18)
f. The reward of the ministry (vv. 19-20)

4. Timothy's report as to the progress of the Thessalonians (3:1-13)

a. Timothy sent to Thessalonica (vv. 1-5)
b. Timothy brings back good tidings of the Thessalonians (vv. 6-13)

II. PRACTICAL—INSTRUCTION CONCERNING THE LIFE CHRISTIANS SHOULD LIVE IN VIEW OF THE IMMINENT RETURN OF THE LORD (Chs. 4-5)

1. Instruction regarding holiness (4:1-8)
2. Instruction regarding love of the brethren (4:9-10)
3. Instruction regarding conduct toward those outside the church (4:11-12)

4. Instruction regarding the rapture of the saints
   (4:13-18)
5. Instruction regarding the revelation of Christ
   (His return to reign) (5:1-11)
6. Sundry instructions (5:12-28)

II THESSALONIANS

Introduction

I. AUTHOR

Paul the apostle (1:1; 3:17)

II. RECIPIENTS

The church of the Thessalonians (1:1). For information on Thessalonica, see introduction to I
Thessalonians.

III. DATE

About A.D. 52. Evidently written shortly after I
Thessalonians, as Paul still links Silas and Timothy
with himself. They were not with him for a long
time after his stay in Corinth (Acts 18:5, 18; 19:22);
Silas so far as we know was never with Paul again.
Paul stayed in Corinth for a year and a half, however (Acts 18:11), so this epistle must have been
written during that time.

IV. PURPOSE

Scofield suggests that probably when the messenger who carried I Thessalonians returned and gave
his report, Paul then wrote II Thessalonians.

1. They needed further instruction concerning
   "the coming of the Lord" (2:1) and "the day

of the Lord" (2:2; cf. 1:3 with I Thessalonians 1:3). Had they grown in hope? Evidently not from II Thessalonians 2:2. In I Thessalonians they were concerned because they thought the "dead in Christ" would miss out on the blessing of His coming. In II Thessalonians they are shown to have become confused about the living but suffering saints, thinking that because of their suffering they were already in the opening days of the Great Tribulation. Note that this confusion was not caused simply by misunderstanding, but there was a direct attempt by Satan to deceive them through false teachers and spurious letters (2:2).

2. They also needed encouragement in the midst of severe persecution (1:4-7).

3. They needed exhortation, for some thought perhaps that since the coming of Christ was so near they could stop working (3:10-11); others were disorderly (3:6); all were in danger of growing "weary in well-doing" (3:13).

V. THEME
The day of the Lord (2:2)

VI. KEY VERSES: 1:7b-10

Outline of II Thessalonians
I. ENCOURAGEMENT IN PERSECUTION (Ch. 1)
  1. Introduction (vv. 1-2)

2. Thanksgiving (vv. 3-10)
3. Prayer (vv. 11-12)
   First of four brief prayers in this short epistle.

II. Instruction Regarding "the Day of the Lord" (Ch. 2)
   1. Exhortation as to the present attitude of mind we should have in view of the coming of "the Day of the Lord" (vv. 1-3a)
   2. Clear statement of the order of events and other important details (vv. 3b-12)
   3. Thanksgiving and prayer for the brethren (vv. 13-17)

III. Exhortations with Regard to Proper Conduct While "Waiting for Christ" (Ch. 3)
   1. Request for prayer (vv. 1-2)
   2. The apostle's confidence in the work the Lord is doing with these people (vv. 3-5)
   3. Command concerning the disorderly (vv. 6-15)
   4. Final prayer and closing salutation (vv. 16-18)

I TIMOTHY
Introduction

I. Author
Paul the apostle (1:1).

II. Recipient
Timothy, "my own son in the faith" (1:2; see also 1:18; 6:20. For the history of Timothy, see Acts 16:1-3; 18:5; 19:22; 20:4).

III. DATE

About A.D. 64-65. It seems that Paul was released from his first imprisonment and was free from about A.D. 63 to 67 before being imprisoned again and finally executed. Apparently I Timothy was written during this period of freedom.

IV. PURPOSE

For about a century or more I and II Timothy and Titus have been called "the pastoral epistles," because they were written to young pastors in charge of churches (as distinguished from letters to churches or groups of Christians and to private individuals, such as Philemon). While there are many personal elements, the main purpose is to provide guidance for pastors in official places of leadership.

I Timothy was written:

1. To warn against false teachers (1:3-7; 19-20).
2. To give instruction regarding sound doctrine and church government. The latter not described in detail, but great principles are clearly stated which are to guide the church throughout the age.)

V. THEME

Proper order in the Church

VI. KEY VERSE: 3:15
KEY WORDS: *Doctrine* (*good doctrine, sound doctrine*) —8 times
Teach, teacher—7 times

Godliness—8 times
Good—22 times

Outline of I Timothy

I. SOUND DOCTRINE IN THE CHURCH (Ch. 1)
1. Introduction (vv. 1-2)
2. False doctrine to be rebuked (vv. 3-11)
3. Paul's thankfulness for the true Gospel and for the empowering of God to preach it (vv. 12-17)
4. The charge to Timothy (vv. 18-20)

II. PUBLIC WORSHIP IN THE CHURCH (Ch. 2)
1. Prayer to be made for all men (vv. 1-7)
2. The place of men and women in public worship (vv. 8-15)

III. OFFICERS IN THE CHURCH (Ch. 3)
1. Qualifications of elders (vv. 1-7)
2. Qualifications of deacons (vv. 8-13)
3. The reason for writing these regulations (vv. 14-16)

IV. A GOOD MINISTER IN THE CHURCH (Ch. 4)
1. Warning against apostasy in the latter times (vv. 1-5)
2. The duty of a good minister of Jesus Christ (vv. 6-16)

V. A GOOD PASTOR IN THE CHURCH (Ch. 5)
1. The attitude of a good pastor to various classes (vv. 1-3)
2. The care of aged widows (vv. 4-16) Cf. Acts 6:1

3. Instruction regarding treatment of elders (vv. 17-21)

4. Various personal instructions (vv. 22-25)

VI. CONCLUDING INSTRUCTIONS (Ch. 6)

1. Instruction regarding servants and masters (vv. 1, 2)

2. False teachers and their motives—pride and avarice (vv. 3-10)

3. The course of the true man of God (vv. 11-16)

4. Instruction for the rich (vv. 17-19)

5. Closing charge to Timothy (vv. 20-21)

II TIMOTHY
Introduction

I. AUTHOR

Paul the apostle (1:1)

II. RECIPIENT

Timothy (1:2)

III. DATE

About A.D. 67. Paul is now in prison at Rome again, and writes to Timothy to come to him at once as the time is short (1:8, 16; 4:6, 9-16, 21).

IV. PURPOSE

1. Paul writes to summon his beloved fellow worker Timothy to his side (4:9, 21).

2. Paul writes in order to show Timothy the proper course for a true servant of Jesus Christ in a time of declension and apostasy.

V. THEME

The true minister of Jesus Christ, or "the servant of the Lord" (2:24)

VI. KEY VERSES: 4:1-5

KEY WORD: *good*—5 times

Outline of II Timothy

I. THE TRUE MINISTER NOT TO BE ASHAMED OF THE TESTIMONY OF THE LORD (1:1-14)
1. Introduction (vv. 1-2)
2. Thanksgiving (vv. 3-5)
3. The true minister exhorted to "stir up the gift of God" (vv. 6-10)
4. The example of Paul (vv. 11-12)
5. The true minister exhorted to hold fast to God's truth (vv. 13-14)

II. THE TRUE MINISTER TO BE A "GOOD SOLDIER OF JESUS CHRIST" IN A TIME OF DECLENSION (1:15—2:26)
1. The declension (1:15-13)
2. The true minister's proper course in the midst of such a declension (2:1-26)
   Soldier, athlete, husbandman, workman, vessel unto honor, servant of the Lord.

III. THE TRUE MINISTER WARNED OF APOSTASY IN THE LAST DAYS (3:1—4:5)
1. Description of perilous times in the last days (3:1-9)

   2. The true minister to follow Paul's example (3:10-13)

   3. The true minister to study and preach God's Word regardless of the course of the age (3:14—4:5)

IV. CONCLUSION: THE FAREWELL OF PAUL (4:6-22)

   1. Paul's soon departure (vv. 6-8)

   2. Personal instructions for Timothy (vv. 9-15)

   3. The faithfulness of the Lord to Paul (vv. 16-18)

   4. Closing greetings and benediction (vv. 19-22)

TITUS

Introduction

I. AUTHOR

Paul the apostle (1:1).

II. RECIPIENT

Titus, whom Paul calls "mine own son after the common faith" (1:4). Titus, like Timothy, was a younger minister who was very helpful to Paul in his work for Christ. He is not mentioned in Acts, but is frequently referred to in the Pauline epistles. He was a Gentile, Greek by birth (Gal. 2:3), and was evidently led to Christ by Paul. He accompanied Paul and Barnabus to the Jerusalem council (Acts 15; Gal. 2:1). He was sent by Paul on important missions a number of times and is spoken of by Paul in the highest terms (II Cor. 7:5-7, 13-14; 8:6, 16-23; II Tim. 4:10).

III. Date

About the same time as I Timothy, A.D. 64-65.

IV. Purpose

Titus had been left in Crete (an island in the Mediterranean Sea near Greece) to establish and regulate the churches there (1:5). Just when Paul did this work in Crete is not known, as the only reference to a visit there is in Acts 27:7, and it does not seem he could have done much then. His work there was apparently abruptly cut short, however, and Titus was left to finish it.

1. Paul writes to Titus to give specific instruction as to the kind of men who are qualified to be elders in the churches of Crete.
2. Paul writes to Titus to show the life that should be lived by all those who are saved by God's grace.

V. Theme

The godly life of the believer

VI. Key Verses: 2:11-14

Key Words: *Sound* (doctrine, faith, speech) — 5 times

Good works—6 times

Good—11 times

Outline of Titus

I.   Salutation (1:1-4)

II.   Qualifications of Elders (1:5-9)

III. Warning Against False Teachers (1:10-16)

IV. INSTRUCTIONS FOR VARIOUS CLASSES IN THE CHURCH (2:1—3:11)
1. Instructions for older men (2:1-2)
2. Instructions for older women (2:3)
3. Instructions for young women (2:4-5)
4. Instructions for young men (2:6-8)
5. Instructions for servants (2:9-10)
6. Basis for the above instructions (2:11-15)
7. General instructions for all (3:1-11)

V. PERSONAL CONCLUSION (3:12-15)

PHILEMON

Introduction

I. AUTHOR

Paul the apostle (1:1, 19).

II. RECIPIENT

Philemon, a Christian of Colosse (see vv. 1, 2, 10, cf. Col. 4:9, 17).

III. DATE

Written at the same time as Ephesians and Colossians—A.D. 62—while Paul was in his first imprisonment at Rome.

IV. PURPOSE

Philemon, a wealthy Christian of Colosse, has apparently been robbed by a runaway slave, Onesimus (vv. 10, 11, 16, 18). Onesimus flees to Rome and is there led to the Lord by Paul. Paul then sends him back to Philemon (vv. 12, 15, 16), and writes this

epistle to intercede for him. Onesimus returns with
Tychicus, who carried the letters to the Ephesians
and Colossians. The letter also provides an ideal
example of true Christian tact and courtesy.

V. THEME

Paul intercedes for a runaway slave.

VI. KEY VERSES: 17-19

Outline of Philemon

I. INTRODCTION (vv. 1-7)

II. APPEAL (vv. 8-21)

III. CONCLUSION (vv. 22-25)

HEBREWS

Introduction

I. AUTHOR
   Uncertain.
   1. General opinion of Church since earliest times
      has been that Paul was the author, though
      some have denied this from second century on.
      Arguments for Paul's authorship:
      a. Peter's statement (II Peter 3:15, 16; cf. with
         I Peter 1:1; II Peter 3:1)
      b. Doctrinal teaching in line with what Paul
         writes in other letters (cf. Heb. 5:12-14
         with I Cor. 3:2; Heb. 3:12-19 with I Cor.
         10:1-11; Heb. 10:38 with Rom. 1:17 and
         Gal. 3:11; Heb. 9:15 with Rom. 3:25).
      c. Writer had been in bonds (10:34), wrote
         from Italy (13:24), and was closely associ-
         ated with Timothy (13:23; cf. I Thess. 3:2).
      d. The close typically Pauline (cf. 13:25 with
         Rom. 16:24; I Cor. 16:23, 24; II Cor. 13:14;
         Gal. 6:18; Eph. 6:24; Phil. 4:23; Col. 4:18;
         I Thess. 5:28; II Thess. 3:18; I Tim. 6:21;
         II Tim. 4:22; Titus 3:15; Philem. 25). No
         other writers use "grace" in their endings,
         except II Peter 3:18, where it is used in

sense of Christian experience rather than divine grace bestowed, "grow in grace."

e. Provides last of three commentaries on Habakkuk 2:4, along with Romans and Galatians. Seems God would have used same writer for last of the three as for first two.

2. Objections center around name not being used; the style; the language. Objectors (and this includes many reverent scholars) suggest Luke, Apollos, Barnabas, Philip, Priscilla. Pure speculation (cf. II Tim. 3:16).

II. RECIPIENTS

1. Originally a group of Jewish Christians (as James, I and II Peter). Not Hebrew Christians in general, but a particular group in a certain locality (13:7, 17-19, 22-24)

2. Known by writer personally (5:11, 12; 6:9, 10; 10:32-34; 12:4).

3. Precise locality unknown, but they were familiar with Old Testament and with temple worship, so probably in Palestine.

4. Spiritual condition: had made a profession of faith in Christ (3:1; 4:14; 10:23). Gave some evidence of being truly saved (6:10; 10:32-34). But too much of a tendency to look backward to the old covenant (1:1; 3:5, 6; 7:11; 8:7, etc.). Also a spiritual backwardness and sluggishness that made the writer doubt if some were truly born again (3:12; 5:11-14; 12:25, etc.).

III. DATE

Evidently prior to destruction of temple in A.D. 70, as various texts indicate clearly that the temple worship was still in progress (8:4; 9:6; 10:11; 13:10). Probably A.D. 63-68.

IV. PURPOSE

1. To present the Lord Jesus Christ in His absolute pre-eminence as the final and complete revelation of God. Christ pictured as the Son of God who became incarnate that He might be our great High Priest, the one Mediator between God and men. The only book which deals fully with the priestly ministry of Christ, His superiority over all previous revelations of God, and of the new covenant over the old covenant.

2. To use this fact of the superiority of Christ and the new covenant in His blood as the basis for encouragement and warning to the readers. Immature Christians are encouraged to go on with the Lord and grow in grace. Five parenthetical warnings. Those enlightened concerning the Gospel but having as yet had no real transaction with the Lord are warned lest they should at that point turn back and fail to receive "so great salvation."

V. THEME

Our Great High Priest

VI. KEY VERSE: 4:14

KEY WORDS

Perfection—with verb and adjective used 11 times. Not absolute perfection, but maturity in Christian experience contrasted with carnal, immature walk.

Eternal (and forever) —used 13 times. Emphasizes finality of Christianity with temporary nature of old covenant.

Heaven (*heavens, heavenly*) —16 times. Shows that realities of Christian faith are not earthly in Nature (as those of Judaism largely were) but spiritual.

Better—12 times. Significant. Christ better than angels or greatest of men. Through Him we have a better covenant, a better sacrifice, a better resurrection, etc.

Partakers—7 times. Fellowship and joint participation. We have fellowship with one another and with Christ such as could not be experienced under Judaism. Christian life not theoretical, but an actual living experience.

Having . . . let us; leaving . . . let us. These phrases used several times. Point to importance of going on with the Lord, both to believer and unbeliever. Life lived in accordance with knowledge we have.

Lest—10 times. Warning word, lest we be hearers of the word and not doers.

Faith—31 times (24 times in chapter 11 alone).

Outline of Hebrews

(Taken from Griffith-Thomas, who attributes it to Westcott, Milligan, and Murray.)

I. INTRODUCTION (1:1-4)

II. THE SUPREME GLORY OF THE PERSON OF CHRIST AS THE SON OF GOD (1:5—4:13)

1. His superiority to angels (1:5—2:18)
(Chapter 1 pictures Christ as superior to angels as Son of God; chapter 2 pictures Christ as superior to angels even as Son of Man; as ideal perfect man He shall rule and reign.)
First practical exhortation—against neglect (2:1-4)

2. His superiority to Moses (3:1—4:13)
Moses was the great man through whom the law had been given; the great leader under whom Israel had become a nation. The writer does not belittle Moses, but shows how far superior Christ is.
Second practical exhortation—against unbelief 3:7—4:13)
First the writer warns, "Harden not your hearts." Then, "Today if ye will hear his voice"—the rest that comes from believing His words.

III. THE SUPREME GLORY OF THE PRIESTHOOD OF CHRIST AS SON OF GOD (4:14—10:18)

1. The provisions of the priest (4:14-16)

2. The qualifications of the priest (5:1—6:20)

Third practical exhortation—against apostasy (5:11—6:20)

3. The person of the priest (7:1-28)

4. The work of the priest (8:1—10:18)

IV. THE PERSONAL APPROPRIATION AND PRACTICAL APPLICATION (10:19—13:25)

1. The new life (10:19-39)

Faith (10:19-22)

Hope (10:23)

Love (10:24-25)

Fourth practical exhortation—against willful sin (10:26-39)

"The willful sin in this passage is the definite rejection of His atoning sacrifice" (Ironside).

2. The first encouragement to progress—faith (11:1-40)

3. The second encouragement to progress—hope (12:1-24)

Fifth practical exhortation—against obstinate refusal and disobedience (12:25-29)

4. The third encouragement to progress—love (13:1-17)

5. Personal conclusion (13:18-25)

JAMES

Introduction

For many centuries James, Peter, John and Jude have been called the "general epistles." Just why is uncertain; possibly because of the authorship, the contents, or the recipients.

(See the present writer's book *James—Christian Faith in Action*, Moody Colportage Library, No. 251)

I. AUTHOR

James, called by Paul "the Lord's brother" (Gal. 1:19), a son of Joseph and Mary and, according to the flesh, the half-brother of our Lord Jesus Christ. Note several references to him:

Matthew 13:55—Mentioned first in list of four brethren of Christ, and so apparently the eldest.

John 7:5—Apparently not a believer before the death of Christ.

I Corinthians 15:7; Acts 1:14—After seeing the death and resurrection of Christ, James and the other brethren became firm believers and participated in the prayer meeting between the ascension and Pentecost.

Acts 12:17; 15:13; 21:18—He soon rose to a place of prominence and became the recognized leader of the Church at Jerusalem. In this connection, Paul speaks of him as a "pillar of the church" and director of its activities (Gal. 2:9, 12).

He was a pious, devout man, of sterling Christian character, who truly lived the doctrine he preached.

II. RECIPIENTS

"The twelve tribes which are scattered abroad" (1:1). "The twelve tribes which are of the disper sion" (R.V.). Addressed originally to Jewish *Christians* (2:1), as Hebrews, and I and II Peter. But like other New Testament epistles, also written for Chris tians of all times (II Tim. 3:16, 17).

III. DATE

Generally considered to be the earliest of all New Testament epistles. Written from Jerusalem before James' death (which occurred A.D. 62-63) — possibly about A.D. 45.

IV. PURPOSE

To show that true faith should result in a life of outward piety and good works. It is not a polemic against Paul's epistle to the Romans, as some have imagined. James' epistle was written before Romans and could not be an answer to it. Careful study reveals that there is no conflict between James and Paul. Paul deals primarily with the doctrine of justification before God, which comes not at all through works, but entirely through faith in Christ and His atoning death. James deals primarily with justification before men. He is not disparaging a true heart-faith, but rather is emphasizing the fact

that such a faith should result in a life full of good
works.

V. THEME

True faith produces works. "The theme of James
was pre-eminently that of faith producing works.
James did not argue against faith; he argued for
faith. Recognizing this fact, we turn to consider the
essential message of the letter, and find its central
teaching has a positive and a negative emphasis.
The positive teaching may be summarized thus:
Faith in God produces life according to the will of
God; while the negative teaching is that life contrary
to the will of God denies faith in God" (G. Campbell Morgan).

VI. KEY VERSE: 2:20

KEY WORDS: *Faith*—16 times

Works—15 times

Outline of James

I. FAITH TESTED (Chs. 1-2)

  1. By attitude toward trials from without (1:1-8)
  2. By attitude toward worldly position (1:9-11)
  3. By attitude toward fleshly temptations (1:12-
      18)
  4. By obedience to the Word of God (1:19-27)
      a. Receiving the Word (vv. 19-21)
      b. "Doing" the Word (vv. 22-27)
  5. By attitude toward our fellow men (2:1-13)
  6. By the presence or absence of good works (2:
      14-26)

I PETER
Introduction

I. AUTHOR

The apostle Peter (1:1, 8; 5:1) perhaps the best known of the twelve. He was originally a fisherman of Galilee, who became interested in the preaching of John the Baptist and was later brought to Christ by his brother Andrew who had heard John's testimony. His original name was Simon or Simeon, but he was named Peter by the Lord. He was married.

Many events of his life stand out in our minds: walking on water; great confession followed by Satanic statement; his boast never to forsake Christ followed by his denial; his penitence and dealing with the resurrected Christ. His great sermon of Pentecost and another after healing lame man at beautiful gate. Delivered by angel from imprisonment and execution. Preaching to first Gentiles. Firm testimony for salvation through faith and for Christian liberty at Jerusalem (Acts 15); his denial of Christian liberty by his actions at Antioch (Gal. 2).

II. RECIPIENTS

"The strangers scattered throughout Pontus, Galatia, Cappadocia, Asia, and Bithynia" (1:1, 2). Strangers, "diaspora," Jews who lived outside Palestine and yet looked on it as their native land. But also to Christians everywhere (1:18-19, 23; 2:10, 24, etc.). He speaks to them not as *Jews* but as *Christians*. Remember Peter was especially the apostle to the Jews, as Paul to the Gentiles (Gal. 2:7-8) . (Note: this does not mean that either limited himself exclusively to those groups.)

III. DATE

About A.D. 63. Paul was released from his first imprisonment in Rome about that year. This epistle has a number of similarities to the epistles of Paul, which leads scholars to think that Peter was familiar with Paul's writings (II Peter 3:15 bears this out). Therefore he wrote after Paul's principal epistles had been penned.

IV. PLACE OF WRITING

Babylon (5:13). Does Peter mean literal Babylon on Euphrates, or Rome, or another Babylon? Roman Catholic Church claims this as proof of Peter's being first pope. Very slim evidence. Does not seem he founded the church there or he would be mentioned in Romans or Acts 28. Tradition says he started to flee Rome when persecution became severe under Nero, but saw vision of Lord to whom he said:

"Domine, quo vadis?" ("Lord, whither goest Thou?") The Lord answered, "I go to Rome to be crucified there anew." Peter then returned to suffer martyrdom himself. Seems unlikely that in a clear, plain letter Peter would use a term of mystical symbolism.

V. Purpose

Encouragement to persecuted and suffering Christians (1:6-7; 5:8-9). Peter also foresees more severe trials yet ahead (4:12-13). Note his statement in 5:12. He seeks to give them consolation during the present sufferings and to prepare them for the trials still ahead. This he does by showing them the wonderful hope that lies ahead (1:13), and also by pointing them to the example of Christ (2:21-23). All—husbands, wives, servants, elders, people—are exhorted to fulfill their individual duties and to give the enemies no ground for a true complaint (4:15-16).

VI. Theme

Comfort for suffering Christians.

VII. Key Verses: 4:12, 13

Key Words: *Suffer* and *sufferings*—15 times (also implied about 6 times)

Glory and *glorify*—16 times. Word refers usually to the wonderful hope ahead, the glory that will come; sometimes to glorifying God even now by patient endurance.

Grace—10 times (Note this includes Greek for 2:19, 20; see also 5:12)

Precious—5 times. What are the precious things that we as Christians have even though we may be suffering affliction in the world?

Hope—4 times

Outline of I Peter

I. SUFFERING IN RELATION TO SALVATION (1:1-12)
   1. Salutation (vv. 1-2)
   2. Even though we suffer now ("for a little while") we can rejoice in our wonderful salvation (vv. 3-12)

II. SUFFERING IN RELATION TO HOLINESS OF LIFE (1:13—3:22)
   1. The call to holiness (1:13-21)
   2. The call to love (1:22-25)
   3. The call to growth (2:1-10)
   4. Our conduct as strangers and pilgrims (2:11-12)
   5. Our conduct as citizens (2:13-17)
   6. Our conduct as employees (2:18-20)
   7. The example of Christ (2:21-25)
   8. Proper conduct for wives or husbands (3:1-7)
   9. Proper conduct for all innocent sufferers (3:8-22)

III. THE NEW LIFE CONTRASTED WITH THE OLD (4:1-11)

IV. PARTAKING OF CHRIST'S SUFFERINGS (4:12-19)

V. EXHORTATIONS IN VIEW OF THE LORD'S RETURN (5:1-14)

II PETER
Introduction

I. Author

The apostle Peter (1:1; cf. 1:14 with John 21:18-19). II Peter 1:16-17 pictures the transfiguration (Matt. 17:1-5; see also 3:1).

II. Recipients

Same as in I Peter (II Peter 3:1; "like precious faith," 1:1).

III. Date

"Just before Peter's death; probably A.D. 66. Also after a number of Paul's epistles were written (3:15).

IV. Purpose

To strengthen and confirm believers against attack, but note the attack is quite different from that in I Peter. That epistle centered around persecution and attack from the outside; II Peter deals with attack from the inside from false teachers. Two types of attack like this are mentioned: false teachers who bring in heresies and deny the Lord (2:1-2); scoffers who will scorn the return of the Lord (3:3-4). In spite of these attacks, Peter's word to us is, "Grow in grace" (3:17, 18). Contrast this with "Stand ye fast therein" (I Peter 5:12). If you know Christ, you are "in God's grace," stand fast therein; yes, but even beyond this, "grow" (1:5-7). This especially in view of the imminence of the Lord's return and the consummation of all things (3:11-14).

V. THEME

Warning against false teachers

VI. KEY VERSE: 2:1

KEY WORDS: *Knowledge* (the antidote to false teaching) —6 times

Judgment (on the false teachers) —4 times

VII. COMPARISON WITH II TIMOTHY

Both were written when the writers were at the end of life (II Timothy 4:6; II Peter 1:14). Both express deep confidence in the Lord and assurance of the writer's position in Him. Both deal with apostasy, especially in the "last days."

Outline of II Peter

I. THE FAITHFUL SHEPHERD FEEDS THE SHEEP (Ch. 1).

(See John 21:15-16)

II. THE FAITHFUL SHEPHERD TENDS THE SHEEP (Chs. 2-3).

1. Warning against false teachers (Ch. 2)

2. Warning against scoffers in the last days (3:1-7)

3. Exhortation to holiness of life in view of the day of the Lord (3:8-14)

I JOHN

Introduction

I. AUTHOR

1. Author does not call himself by name, but speaks in first person ("we write" 1:4; "I

write" 2:1). The earliest Christian writers after the apostolic period quote this epistle as from the apostle John. The almost unanimous opinion of the Early Church is that the Gospel and the epistle were the legacies of John in his old age to the Church.

2. Internal evidence is overwhelming that John wrote the epistle. The writer was an eyewitness of our Lord (1:1-3). Many words and phrases used in I John which are used nowhere else in New Testament except in Gospel of John. Samples: "the Word" (John 1:1; I John 1:1; Rev. 19:13); joy full (John 16:24 and I John 1:4); to do the truth (John 3:21 and I John 1:6); to have sin (John 9:41 and I John 1:8); Paraclete (Gr., John 14:16 and I John 2:1); the true light (John 1:9 and I John 2:8); new commandment (John 13:34 and I John 2:8); little children, begotten of God; no man hath beheld God at any time; to overcome the world, etc.

II. RECIPIENTS

1. Not addressed to any particular local church, and so along with James, Peter, and Jude has been called one of the "catholic" or "general" epistles from earliest times. Probably means that these epistles were not addressed to any particular local church or individual.

2. Probably first sent to churches scattered throughout Asia Minor where John had ministered (see Rev. 1). Evidently the writer was familiar with the first readers. However, it is simply addressed to those "that believe on the name of the Son of God" (5:13). These believers are divided into three classes (2:13); "fathers" those mature in the Christian life; "young men," those who have not been Christians very long but are advancing nicely; "little children," those who have just recently been saved (*paidia*). Observe another word is used to address all these as children (*teknia*).

III. DATE

Probably around A.D. 90

IV. PURPOSE

Gospel of John—"Have life" (John 20:31)

I John—"Know that ye have life" (5:13)

"That your joy may be full" (1:4)

"That ye sin not" (2:1)

So the epistle is written to give assurance to those who have believed on Christ, and to show us how we can walk in close fellowship with the Lord so that we may "sin not" and that our joy "may be full."

V. THEME

The family of God

VI. KEY VERSES: 5:12

KEY WORDS

Know—about 35 times (Two Greek words; cf. John 17:3; also I John 2:3; 4:13; 3:5; 5:13, 20).

World—23 times. Almost always in evil sense——our enemy (2:15-17).

Love—21 times

Light—6 times

If we truly *know* God and are in fellowship with Him, then we will walk in *light* and walk in *love*. We will not *love* the *world*.

VII. CHARACTERISTICS OF EPISTLE
   1. Simple language but deep truths
   2. Sharp contrasts (e.g., 2:4-5; 5:19; 1:5; 3:14; 4:20; 2:15; 2:22)
   3. Emphasis on incarnation—humanity of Christ Gospel emphasizes His deity
   4. No Old Testament quotations
   5. Familiar truths repeated and re-emphasized

Outline of I John

INTRODUCTION (1:1-4)

I. GOD IS LIGHT (1:5—2:29)
   1. Walking in the light (1:5-10)
   2. Christ our Advocate (2:1-11)
   3. The family of God (2:12-17)
   4. Christ and Antichrist (2:18-29)

II. GOD IS LOVE (3:1—4:21)
   1. Prepared for His coming (3:1-3)
   2. Two families (3:4-12)

3. The love life (3:13-24)
4. The Spirit of truth and the spirit of error (4: 1-10)
5. Abiding in love (4:11-21)

III. GOD IS LIFE (5:1-21)
1. Life in the Son (5:1-12)
2. Confidence in Him (5:13-21)

II JOHN
Introduction

I. AUTHOR

Author signs himself as "the elder." Some difference of opinion in Early Church as to author, but thought to be John. The epistle has strong internal evidence pointing to John: seven or eight verses of II John are either identical with or very similar to verses in I John.

II. RECIPIENT

"The elect lady and her children"

Three theories offered:

1. A local church and its members
2. The Church as a whole and its members (see v. 13)
3. Most natural explanation: an individual Christian lady. Both words ("elect"—*electra;* and "lady"—*cyria*) have been taken for her name. The Authorized Version is preferable.

Remember that like other epistles the truth is intended for all Christians.

III. DATE
  Probably around A.D. 90.

IV. PURPOSE
  1. To give this lady a good report concerning her
     children (v. 4).
  2. To warn and instruct her with regard to com-
     promising with false teachers. She is told how
     to avoid being deceived (v. 9), and how to
     treat deceivers (vv. 10-11).

V. THEME
  Warning against receiving deceivers

VI. KEY VERSES 9,10
    KEY WORD: *Truth*—5 times

Outline of II John

I.   WALK IN TRUTH (vv. 1-4)
II.   LOVE ONE ANOTHER (vv. 5-6)
III. RECEIVE NOT DECEIVERS (vv. 7-11)
IV.   FIND JOY IN FELLOWSHIP (vv. 12-13)

III JOHN
Introduction

I. AUTHOR
  Same as II John—"the elder." Letters very similar and evidently written by same author. No
reason to believe it was not the apostle John.

II. RECIPIENT
  "The well-beloved Gaius." A faithful Christian

man, convert of John. We know nothing more about him or about where he lived.

III. DATE

Around A.D. 90

IV. PURPOSE

The apostle had sent certain faithful servants of God to minister to this church. Diotrephes, a leader in the church, refused to receive these faithful ministers and to have fellowship with them. Beyond this, he threatened to cast out of the church those who did have fellowship with these brethren. Note the contrast between II and III John: II John warns against having fellowship with those who are false teachers and deny the "doctrine of Christ." III John warns against refusing to have fellowship with those who are true believers and witnesses for Christ.

Compare: I John—These "went out" (2:19).

II John—These want to get in (v. 10).

III John—These want to cast out those who should be in (v. 10).

There is also a word of commendation to Gaius and a prayer for improvement in his physical health.

I John deals with assurance in salvation.

II John instructs us to walk in the truth and not have fellowship with those who deny teachings of Bible.

III John instructs us to have fellowship with all who do believe the Gospel.

V. THEME
Admonition to receive true believers

VI. KEY VERSE: 8
   KEY WORD: *Truth* (with *true*) —7 times

Outline of III John

Book hinges around three men: Gaius, Diotrephes, Demetrius.

I. GAIUS (vv. 1-8)
Walking in the truth (vv. 1-4)
A fellow helper to the truth (vv. 5-8)

II. DIOTREPHES (vv. 9-11)
The evil and arrogant "church boss"

III. DEMETRIUS (v. 12)
Has "a good report of the truth"

IV. CLOSING GREETING (vv. 13-14)

JUDE
Introduction

I. AUTHOR

Jude (literally, Judas), who describes himself as "the servant of Jesus Christ, and brother of James" (v. 1). He was another brother of our Lord according to the flesh (see Matthew 13:55; Galatians 1:19). It is notable to observe that neither he nor James even mention their earthly relationship to the Lord Jesus, but simply designate themselves as "bond servants of Jesus Christ." Jude also mentions the fact that he is the brother of James. Evidently James (whether still alive or not) was much better known than Jude. Distinguish Jude or "Judas" from an apostle by the same name (John 14:22), and of course from Judas Iscariot. A common name among the Jews (Greek form of Hebrew Judah). Jude was not an apostle (vv. 17-18).

As in the case of several of these last books of the Bible, a few in the Early Church were doubtful of its place in the canon. However, it was immediately received by the vast majority of Christians, and within a short time its place in the Bible was accepted by all.

II. RECIPIENTS

Addressed to believers in general: "sanctified . . . preserved . . . called" (v. 1). Since James is mentioned, some think it may possibly have first been sent to the same ones to whom James wrote: "twelve tribes of the dispersion."

III. DATE

Must have been written after II Peter (since he quotes that book, vv. 17, 18). If II Peter written in A.D. 66, then Jude sometime later, perhaps A.D. 70-80.

IV. PURPOSE

Jude tells us frankly that he at first intended just writing a letter concerning "the common salvation." But the Holy Spirit led him to write of quite a different subject. Why? Because of the great danger from false teachers who had "crept in" ("sneaked in," Williams) (v. 4). A solemn warning is urgent.

These false teachers are clearly described so that
the true Christian may be on his guard against them.
At the same time real believers are comforted and
encouraged (vv. 20-25).

V. THEME
   Contending for the faith

VI. KEY VERSE: 3
    KEY WORD: *Ungodly*—6 times

VII. SPECIAL NOTE
   Relationship of Jude to II Peter. The message of
Jude about these false teachers is very similar in
words, ideas and Old Testament illustrations to II
Peter 2:3—3:4. From the statement in Jude 17, 18,
it is easy to see that Jude was written after II Peter
and that the writer was familiar with Peter's letter.
Note some distinctions: (1) Peter says these false
teachers will come.   Jude says they *have come*—
crept in, and he says that they "were written of before in the past" (literally v. 4) ; evidently another
reference to Peter's letter.   (2) In Jude also the
picture of these false teachers is even darker than
that given in II Peter.

Outline of Jude

I.   SALUTATION (vv. 1-2)

II. REASON FOR WRITING (vv. 3-4)

III. EXAMPLES FROM THE PAST SHOWING GOD'S
     HATRED OF SIN AND JUDGMENT ON UNBELIEF (vv.
     5-11)

   1. Example of Israel in the wilderness (v. 5)

2. The angels who fell (v. 6)
3. Sodom and Gomorrah (v. 7)
4. Lawlessness (vv. 8-10)
5. Cain (v. 11a)
6. Balaam (v. 11b)
7. Core (Korah) (v. 11c)

IV. THE FALSE TEACHERS CHARACTERIZED AND THEIR DOOM PICTURED (vv. 12-19)

V. EXHORTATION AND CONSOLATION FOR TRUE BELIEVERS (vv. 20-25)

REVELATION

Introduction

I. AUTHOR

Four times stated to be John (1:1, 4, 9; 22:8). Early Church fathers attributed it to the apostle John. Some later writers denied this, but their antagonism to the book was chiefly on the ground of its doctrine. The only well-known John was the apostle; so if some other writer by the same name had written this book, he would have distinguished himself if he had been an honest man.

Internal evidence—strong. Certain significant words and phrases bind it to the Gospel and the epistles: *the Word* (John 1:1-14; I John 1:1; Revelation 19:13); *Lamb of God* (John 1:29, 36; used 29 times in Revelation); *dwell*—tabernacle (John 1:14; same Greek word used only here and four times in Revelation). Prophecy of Zechariah 12:10 quoted in John 19:37 and Revelation 1:7. Other words, like *overcome, true,* etc., used in John, I John and Revelation. Swete states that out of 913 words used in Revelation, 416 occur in the Gospel of John.

Author also has intimate knowledge of churches in Asia Minor. Tradition very strong that John spent his old age in Ephesus and also worked with surrounding churches.

II. RECIPIENTS

The seven churches of Asia (1:4, 11; 2:1 ff; 22:
16). Also for all the servants of Christ (1:1; 22:6),
and for any person saved or unsaved who will read
and heed it (1:3; 3:20; 22:7, 17-19).

III. DATE

Probably about A.D. 96

IV. PLACE

Isle of Patmos (1:9 cf. 6:9 and 20:4). John sent
there as a punishment for his preaching. A rough,
bare island, eight miles long and one mile wide, in
Aegean Sea, between what is now Greece and Tur-
key. Worst criminals there worked in mines.

V. PURPOSE

1. To give the final truth about Jesus Christ—the
   unveiling. This book contains an unveiling of
   the person, power and purpose of Jesus Christ.
   Revelation—apocalypse—unveiling.
2. To give instruction, encouragement and rebuke to the professing Church. This especially true of chapters 2 and 3, but also of the
   whole book (see 22:16).

VI. THEME

The revelation of Jesus Christ (1:1)

VII. KEY VERSE: 1:19 (contains a threefold out-
line)

KEY WORDS: *I saw* (with *I beheld, I looked*—
49 times

Seven (and *seventh*) —59 times
(Note seven-fold structure of book)
Angel—70 times
Lamb—29 times

VIII. Schools of Interpretation
  1. Preterist view. Word (Latin) means "to pass by." Book relates events already past when John wrote. History relating to the fall of Jerusalem and the reign of Nero set forth in symbolic form (Held by Stuart, etc.).
  2. Historical interpretation. Book contains a detailed prophecy of Church history from John's time to end of world. Seals, trumpets, vials follow chronologically, and all picture Church history (Held by Barnes, Vitringa, etc.).
  3. Futurist view. Book refers to events yet future which will be fulfilled just prior to and at time of second advent. All premillennialists hold this view, with minor variations.
  4. Spiritual view. More recent interpretation. Little attempt to interpret individual figures: book simply symbolic of age-long struggle between right and wrong, showing right to be at last triumphant (Held by A. T. Robertson; amillennialists in general).

IX. Characteristics of Book
  1. Highly pictorial form of writing
  2. Events not portrayed in strict chronological order

3. Large use of Old Testament Scriptures
4. Striking use of number 7

Outline of Revelation

I.   THE VISION OF THE GLORIOUS CHRIST (Ch. 1)

II. THE LETTERS TO THE SEVEN CHURCHES (Chs. 2-3)

   1. Principles of interpretation

     a. Each letter applied directly to a church then in existence

     b. Letters can be applied to churches anywhere, where similar conditions occur

     c. Also to individuals

     d. Prophetic interpretation: each letter represents also a period of Church history, from time of John to return of Christ

   2. Features of the letters

     a. Address

     b. Description of writer

     c. Commendation of good works

     d. Complaint

     e. Exhortation

     f. Threat

     g. Promise

(Note carefully places where any one of these is omitted.)

III. HEAVENLY SCENES (Chs. 4-5)

   1. Worship of God (Ch. 4)

   2. Worship of the Lamb (Ch. 5)

IV.   The Seven Seals (Chs. 6-7)

V.   The Seven Trumpets (Chs. 8-11)

VI.   Important Persons of the Last Days (Chs. 12-14)

VII. The Seven Vials (Chs. 15-16)

VIII. The Fall of Babylon (Chs. 17-18)

IX.   Events from the Fall of Babylon to the Eternal State (Chs. 19-22)

———————————